CW00645861

THE AGE OF GRACE

THE AGE OF GRACE

CHARIS IN EARLY GREEK POETRY

BONNIE MacLACHLAN

PRINCETON UNIVERSITY PRESS

PRINCETON, NEW JERSEY

Library of Congress Cataloging-in-Publication Data

MacLachlan, Bonnie.
The age of grace : charis in early Greek poetry / Bonnie
MacLachlan.
p.   cm.
Includes bibliographical references and index.
ISBN 0-691-06974-3
1. Greek poetry—History and criticism.   2. Grace (Aesthetics) in
literature.   3. Grace (Theology) in literature.   4. Literature and
society—Greece.   5. Charis (The Greek word).   I. Title.

PA3095.M33 1993   881'.01938—dc20   92-37031

For John

χάρις χάριν γάρ ἐστιν ἡ τίκτουσ' ἀεί

CONTENTS

viii CONTENTS

LIST OF ILLUSTRATIONS

ACKNOWLEDGMENTS

T HIS BOOK began as a doctoral thesis; its roots go back a dozen years or more. In retrospect the time that I have been engaged with χάρις seems a major part of my life, because those years include my academic apprenticeship: Just as the memory of our adolescence looms large in later life, so is it also with our scholarly coming of age. There are many people to thank for their contribution to the foundations, and I have deep pleasure in thanking them, and in offering them some return for their efforts. The German term *Doktorvater* captures an important truth, but there are "Doktoronkels" and "Doktortanten" as well.

The late Willy Borgeaud was the first to draw me into the beguiling world of Pindar, and the first to propose χάρις to me as a worthwhile subject of study. My thesis was written at the University of Toronto under the constantly challenging but unwavering encouragement of Leonard Woodbury; after his death in 1985 the supervision was carried on in a different but still constantly supportive style by Emmet Robbins. I also profited from discussions with Douglas Gerber and Desmond Conacher at this stage. These were my direct mentors, and my gratitude to them is great. But I am also grateful to others who surrounded me with encouragement in those years—Elaine Fantham, Alex Dalzell, Gilbert Bagnani, Stephan Kresic, Pierre Laberge. Early drafts of parts of the thesis were read to meetings of the Société d'études anciennes du Québec in Ottawa in 1982, to the Association canadienne française pour l'avancement des sciences in Chicoutimi in 1984, and to the Classical Association of Canada in Vancouver in 1983 and in Montréal in 1985. I am grateful to the audiences of these occasions for their comments. It is appropriate also to express gratitude to the University of Toronto, the Ontario Graduate Scholarship Programme, and the Margaret McWilliams Memorial Scholarship foundation, all of which at different times gave financial support to my doctoral work.

Sir Hugh Lloyd-Jones read my thesis and urged me to make a book of it. I am grateful for his urging. Joanna Hitchcock of Princeton University Press was an enthusiastic supporter of the project, and the anonymous readers appointed by the Press gave some excellent suggestions. The library of the American Academy in Rome was an important resource for me during the first stage of the revision of the manuscript.

For the most part I have prepared the book while discharging professorial duties in the Department of Classical Studies at the University of Western Ontario. It would be hard to imagine a more welcoming and supportive group of colleagues. I must mention in particular the unfailing material help and professional advice I have received from Christopher Brown, who has been a constant sounding board for matters both large and small. Douglas Gerber has been a genial ἐπίσκοπος since the days of my thesis supervision, and I have benefited greatly from his editorial and bibliographical acuity. The Faculty of Arts has been generous with financial support for computer equipment and for other assistance. Anna Rosenberg, Mary MacLachlan, Franco di Angelis, Dick Shroyer, Jane Cere, Lisa Micheelsen, Nancy Prior, Carrie Galsworthy, Dianne Yates, and Jim Hill have all helped, in one way or another, with the preparation of the final manuscript. Emmet Robbins of the University of Toronto has read the manuscript and provided me with useful suggestions for its final presentation. The careful scrutiny given to the text by Marta Steele of the Press was invaluable. It goes without saying that I take responsibility for any errors that remain.

In sustained scholarly undertakings a professional κοινωνία is vital. But the abiding support of a family has been equally indispensable for me, and I must thank Chris, Jeremy, John Gilbert, Doug, and Anne for their absolute constancy during the various stages of this project.

Above all, I thank my husband, John Thorp, who knows all about *charis*.

ἐγὼ δὲ κέ τοῖς ἰδέω χάριν ἤματα πάντα

Bonnie MacLachlan
London, Ontario
June 1992

A NOTE ON USAGE

THE AGE OF GRACE is intended to be accessible to readers without training in Greek as well as to classicists. I have therefore transliterated Greek words when they appear in the text and translated them when they first occur. The principal words can also be found in the glossary. In the notes, however, particularly when the discussion is of a philological nature, I have used the untransliterated Greek. My regular practice has been to use the Latinized version of Greek proper names, unless the Greek version is in common use.

EDITIONS AND ABBREVIATIONS

BECAUSE *The Age of Grace* covers a broad spectrum of ancient poetic texts, many of which are fragmentary and published in several editions, I list below the editions from which I have cited the principal authors or texts. For the less common ones, or those cited infrequently, I have given an abbreviated reference to the source in the text. For the full reference, see the List of Abbreviations (below).

Unless otherwise stated, the translations are my own.

Editions

Aeschylus: *Aeschylus. Septem Quae Supersunt Tragoediae*, ed. D. Page, Oxford 1972.

Alcaeus: *Sappho et Alcaeus*, ed. E.-M. Voigt, Amsterdam 1971.

Alcman: *Poetarum Melicorum Graecorum Fragmenta*, ed. M. Davies, Oxford 1991.

Anacreon: *Poetae Melici Graeci*, ed. D. Page, Oxford 1962.

Antimachus: *Iambi et Elegi Graeci Ante Alexandrum Cantati*, vol. 2, ed. M. L. West, Oxford 1972.

Archilochus: *Iambi et Elegi Graeci Ante Alexandrum Cantati*, vol. 1², ed. M. L. West, Oxford 1989.

Bacchylides: (Odes) *Die Lieder des Bakchylides*, ed. H. Maehler, Leiden 1982.

————: (Dithyrambs) *Bacchylides*, ed. H. Maehler, post B. Snell, Leipzig 1970.

Cypria: *Poetae Epici Graeci. Testimonia et Fragmenta*, ed. A. Bernabé, Leipzig 1987.

Dionysius Chalcus: *Iambi et Elegi Graeci Ante Alexandrum Cantati*, vol. 2, ed. M. L. West, Oxford 1972.

Hesiod: (*Opera et Dies*) *Hesiod. Works and Days*, ed. M. L. West, Oxford 1978.

————: (*Theogony*) *Hesiod. Theogony*, ed. M. L. West, Oxford 1966.

————: (fragments) *Fragmenta Hesiodea*, ed. R. Merkelbach and M. L. West, Oxford 1967.

Homer: (*Iliad*) *Homeri Opera*[3], ed. D. B. Monro and T. W. Allen, Oxford 1920.

————: (*Odyssey*) *Homeri Opera*[2], ed. T. W. Allen, Oxford 1919.

Homeric Hymn to Demeter: *Homeri Opera*[2], ed. T. W. Allen, Oxford 1930.

Ibycus: *Poetarum Melicorum Graecorum Fragmenta*, ed. M. Davies, Oxford 1991.

Pindar: (Odes) *Pindarus. Pars I. Epinicia*, ed. H. Maehler, post B. Snell, Leipzig 1987.

————: (Fragments) *Pindarus. Pars II: Fragmenta. Indices*, ed. H. Maehler, Leipzig 1989.

Praxilla: *Poetae Melici Graeci*, ed. D. Page, Oxford 1962.

Sappho: *Sappho et Alcaeus*, ed. E.-M. Voigt, Amsterdam 1971.

Semonides: *Iambi et Elegi Graeci Ante Alexandrum Cantati*, vol. 2, ed. M. L. West, Oxford 1972.

Stesichorus: *Poetarum Melicorum Graecorum Fragmenta*, ed. M. Davies, Oxford 1991.

Thucydides: *Thucydidis Historiae*[2], ed. H. S. Jones and I. E. Powell, Oxford 1942.

Xenophanes: *Iambi et Elegi Graeci Ante Alexandrum Cantati*, vol. 2, ed. M. L. West, Oxford 1972.

Abbreviations

A & A	Antike und Abendland
ABSA	Annual of the British School at Athens
Acharn.	Acharnians (Aristophanes)

A Class	Acta Classica
AJA	American Journal of Archaeology
AJAH	American Journal of Ancient History
AJP	American Journal of Philology
Amat.	Amatorius (Plutarch)
Ann Soc	L'Année sociologique
Ant	Die Antike: Zeitschrift für Kunst und Kultur
Astron.	Astronomia (ps.-Hesiod)
Athen.	Athenaeus
BCH	Bulletin de correspondance hellénique
BICS	Bulletin of the Institute of Classical Studies
CA	Classical Antiquity
Carm. Conv.	Carmina Convivialia (anon.)
Cat.	Catalogue of Women (Hesiod)
Charm.	Charmides (Plato)
CJ	Classical Journal
CP	Classical Philology
CQ	Classical Quarterly
CR	Classical Review
CW	Classical World
de Mus.	de Musica (ps.-Plutarch)
DK	Diels-Kranz. Die Fragmente der Vorsokratiker (1951)
Dr	Drachmann. Scholia Vetera in Pindari Carmina (1903–1927)
EMC/ CV	Echos du monde classique/Classical Views
Ep.	Epistulae (Philostratus)
Et. Gen.	Etymologicum Genuinum
FGrH	Die Fragmente der Griechischen Historiker
GRBS	Greek, Roman and Byzantine Studies
H. Ap.	Homeric Hymn to Apollo
H. Dem.	Homeric Hymn to Demeter
Hipp.	Hippolytus (Euripides)
HSCP	Harvard Studies in Classical Philology
IA	Iphigenia in Aulis (Euripides)
ICS	Illinois Classical Studies
Isth.	Isthmian Odes (Pindar)

IT	Iphigenia among the Taurians (Euripides)
JHS	Journal of Hellenic Studies
JWI	Journal of the Warburg and Courtauld Institutes
Ktema	Ktèma. Civilisations de l'Orient, de la Grèce et de Rome antiques
L-S	(Leutsch and Schneidewin) Corpus Paroemiographorum Graecorum
LSJ	(Liddell, Scott, and Jones [Oxford 1940]) Greek-English Lexicon
Lys.	Lysis (Plato)
Mnem	Mnemosyne
Mor.	Moralia (Plutarch)
NE	Nicomachean Ethics (Aristotle)
Nem.	Nemean Odes (Pindar)
OC	Oedipus at Colonus (Sophocles)
Oec.	Oeconomicus (Xenophon)
OED	Oxford English Dictionary
Ol.	Olympian Odes (Pindar)
Op.	Opera et Dies (Works and Days [Hesiod])
Or.	Orationes (Himerius)
Pae.	Paeans (Pindar)
Paus.	Pausanias
PCPS	Proceedings of the Cambridge Philological Society
PMG	Poetae Melici Graeci (ed. Page)
Pyth.	Pythian Odes (Pindar)
QUCC	Quaderni Urbinati di Cultura Classica
RBPh	Revue belge de philologie et d'histoire
RE	Real-Encyclopädie der klassischen Altertumswissenschaft
REG	Revue des études grecques
Rhet.	Rhetoric (Aristotle)
SDHI	Studi et Documenta Historiae et Iuris
SIG	Sylloge inscriptionum graecarum
Stud Gen	Studium generale
Studi Clas	Studii Clasice
Symp.	Symposium (Plato)

TAPA   Transactions and Proceedings of the
         American Philological Association
Theog.   Theogonia (Theogony [Hesiod])
TPS   Transactions of the Philological Society
ZPE   Zeitschrift für Papyrologie und Epigraphik

THE AGE OF GRACE

Chapter One

INTRODUCTION

T HE WORD *grace* has a perplexing variety of meanings. Religious people speak of the grace of God, and
they may say grace before and after meals, hoping by
this and other means to remain in a state of grace. And in
secular speech dancers and antelopes are graceful; host-
esses are gracious, and so, in the language of real estate, are
their homes. The three Graces are familiar ancient divinities
whose purpose and purview has remained puzzling; they
are decorative, at the least, as are grace notes in a melody.
Dukes and archbishops (whether decorative or not) are addressed as "Your Grace," and we seek to remain in our
employers' or superiors' good graces, or, if we have fallen
from grace, to ingratiate ourselves anew. Then there are also
gratuitous cruelty, instant gratification, and hearty congrat-
ulations. What, we might legitimately ask, links these very
diverse meanings and uses of *grace* and its cognates?

The Greek word which we regularly translate as "grace"
is *charis*. Like *grace*, *charis* is found in an impressive array of
contexts in Greek literature. However, it enjoys a prominence, especially in the archaic poetry, that far outstrips that
of *grace*, particularly since the emergence of our secular culture. No serious reader of early Greek poetry can avoid the
fact that *charis* dominates the literary portrayal of life during
the archaic age. It was "the age of grace." *Charis* flickered
when beautiful women sparkled; soldiers brought *charis* to
their commanders on the battlefield or expected to win it
when they fought well; *charis* graced appropriate behavior
and speech and was a distinguishing mark of nobility; it was

at the center of the feast; in the verses of the love poets it sat upon the hair or the eyes of the beloved. For the epinician poets it crowned that moment of supreme glory when the athlete won and was celebrated in song. Indeed, it would seem that for the early Greeks *charis* was present at all the high moments of life. And at death one faced the dreary prospect of the disappearance of *charis*. Just what was the *charis* experience, the sensation that clearly brought the greatest enjoyment to the early Greeks? This book is an attempt to reconstruct this experience. The evidence for the reconstruction is literature, and the literature will itself be illuminated by the reconstruction.

If we were to begin by looking at the linguistic history of the word *charis*, it would immediately be apparent that the idea of pleasure is deeply embedded in the word. The Indo-European root *ǵher- ("pleasure") is parent of *charis* and its cognates *chairein, chara,* etc.[1] But the etymology of a word must always be tested against current usage, and, judging from the semantic field represented by the use of *charis* above, "pleasure" is necessary to, but insufficient as, a definition of the word. Although pleasure is involved in all of these instances, it is pleasure of a specific kind: Clearly other Greek words that denoted pleasure, like *hêdonê* or *chara,* cannot readily be substituted for *charis*.

In a dissertation for the University of Marburg in 1908 entitled ΧΑΡΙΣ (Charis), Otto Löw attempted to identify the special feature of that pleasure which is *charis*. *Charis* for the early Greeks, he argued, was something that brought joy, a *factum laetificans*. This is distinct from a pleasurable state of mind, which would have been described as *chara*. *Charis* is not passive but a *uis laetificatrix* (a pleasure-bearing power).

There were, of course, divine dispensers of this pleasure-bearing power, the Charites. These Löw referred to as *deae*

---

[1] Pokorny I (1959) 440–41; cf. Chantraine (1968) s.v. χάϱις and Frisk (1960) s.v. χαίϱω.

laetificatrices (pleasure-bestowing divinities). The pleasure they conferred was always of a social nature, and this allows us to make a further refinement upon Löw's definition. In distributing beauty, the Charites fostered human or divine interaction through physical allurement. In cult they were worshiped first as fertility goddesses, then venerated for the blessings they brought to the social order as it developed, becoming patrons of youth, of marriage, of healing, and later of the benefits conferred by the city-state. In praise poetry they awarded the *charis* of undying fame to a successful athlete, reciprocating the glory he had brought to the community. Their social importance was familiar to Aristotle, who advised the erection of a temple to the Charites in a prominent place in the city, to ensure reciprocal giving, for this, he says, is the distinguishing feature of *charis* (*NE* 5.1133a). From the Charites, then, we learn that *charis*-pleasure was not private: It entailed enjoyment that was mutual, reciprocal.

This reciprocal return was of course present in the phrase *charin oida*, lit. "I know the favor," words commonly used to express gratitude or thanks (the acknowledgment of the favor) as early as Homer. But even in this expression *charis* retained its active force: It was not merely a passive state of mind, a grateful feeling, but a gesture of response and thus essentially social in its setting.[2] In *Iliad* 14, to advance her

---

[2] Most scholars agree that the phrase χάριν εἰδέναι in early Greek literature denoted an active response as well as a (passive) state of mind. Hewitt 1927, 142–61, argued that the Greeks before ca. 400 B.C.E. did not distinguish the *feeling* of gratitude from the result of this feeling, namely, a concrete act, a gesture of kindness in return. We do not make this distinction either. Our feeling grateful, for example, is inseparable from our expressing this with some form of thanks. However, the important point is that in the early Greek world the expression would take concrete form. The whole experience is a continuum and identified by one word, *charis*. There is a similar reluctance, at least in Homer, to distinguish between the description of an organ of perception and the thing perceived. The whole is one event. See Snell 1953, ch. 1. On χάριν εἰδέναι see Löw 1908, 6, 10; and Scott 1983, 11.

designs following her seduction of Zeus, Hera asks the sleep-god Hypnos if he will lull Zeus to sleep after their lovemaking. If he agrees, she will "acknowledge the favor for all time:"

" Υπνε, ἄναξ πάντων τε θεῶν πάντων τ' ἀνθρώπων,
ἠμὲν δή ποτ' ἐμὸν ἔπος ἔκλυες, ἠδ' ἔτι καὶ νῦν
πείθευ· ἐγὼ δέ κέ τοι ἰδέω χάριν ἤματα πάντα.

Hypnos, lord of all gods and all men,
As you once listened to me, so even now
Be persuaded. I then will acknowledge the favor for all time.

Il. 14.233–35

Further, she will present him with tempting gifts (238). The favor will be requited not only with her recollection of the favor, but with a concrete expression of this. When Hypnos still expresses a reluctance to deceive the king of the gods, Hera offers him the gift he cannot refuse, one of the Charites, Pasithea, "whom he has desired for a long time" (276). The repetition of "for all time" in both passages links the long duration of Hypnos' desire with the enduring pleasure he will award her by his favor. In turn, her gift of gratitude will fulfil his desire, with one of the Charites. The lasting nature of the pleasure experienced by both underscores the *charis*-sequence. Her abiding *charis* will deliver to him his long-desired Charis.

The active force in Hera's promise is still alive in the phrase *charin eidenai* when it occurs in the Theognidean collection. "If you experience some great good thing from me and don't acknowledge the *charis*," says the poet, "may you come to my house next time and find yourself empty-handed" (958). To neglect to return a favor is to ensure that you will be cut off from social interchange, left alone and without a return gift.

Charis bound people together in the archaic Greek world, through the experience of pleasure. Before the Greeks became citizens of a *polis*, when new and more complex levels of loyalty and obligation became operative, the distribution of favors and good behavior—such things as went by the name of *charis*—was enforced with a vigor that is unknown to us. We are familiar with charity that is voluntary and giving that is selfless. For the early Greeks, *charis* was never self-denying but, by the same token, was never confined to the self. The exchange of *charis*-favors was founded upon a very general psychological phenomenon, the disposition to return pleasure to someone who has given it. This pleasure exchange was accepted as a serious social convention, and like *xenia* (the requital of gifts and hospitality which protected travelers in the early Greek world) the *charis*-convention amounted to a *lex talionis*, but of a positive sort. A benefaction called for a suitable return, and reprisals might be taken when the anticipated reciprocity did not occur. The Greeks nearly lost the Trojan War because Achilles withdrew from the fighting, charging that he had not received the *charis* that was his due (*Il.* 9.316).

This reciprocity in which *charis* participated has received a flurry of attention in recent years, by scholars who approach the subject from various disciplines—social anthropology, sociology, economics, and archaeology. With the turn of this century came an intellectual break with a belief in the consummate superiority of the Greeks. Concurrent with the arrival in Western Europe of data provided by the new field of comparative anthropology came a willingness to recognize in archaic and even classical Greece social practices parallel to those in cultures that were commonly designated as primitive.

One of the most universally entrenched practices was the reciprocal gift-exchange, a pattern that became well-known to classical scholars through Marcel Mauss' "Essai sur le don" (1923–24). Moses Finley documented the cardinal role played by gift-giving in the *Odyssey* (1978). Mauss' work received the avid attention of the French structuralists, who were busily applying a new method of analysis to Greek literature, myth, ritual, and social practices. Louis Gernet (1948) pointed to the emotional charge that items received when they became part of a reciprocal exchange. He demonstrated the collective origins of the exchange, tribal communal feasts at which marriages were arranged, where honor and status were preserved through the gift exchange. As Gernet noted, the same honor-bound reciprocal exchange that operated between people and gods can be found in Greek literature from Homer to Euripides and is described as the "bearing," "mingling," etc. of *charis* (1928, 313–59).

In the United States, Karl Polanyi's studies of patterns of economic exchange in primitive societies (1957)[3] encouraged a new examination of the early Greek world by economic as well as social anthropologists. M. D. Sahlins (1972) isolated three categories for the economic exchange and distribution systems of pre-market civilizations which have received considerable attention: (i) generalized reciprocity (close to our altruism), (ii) balanced reciprocity (an equivalent exchange), and (iii) negative reciprocity (stealing, plundering, etc.). These categories have been applied to the Homeric world by W. Donlan (1989, 1982a, 1982b, 1981), to Solon's Attica by T. W. Gallant (1982), and to Pindar by R. Compagner (1988). Only balanced reciprocity interests us in a study of *charis*, for it is the only one that is strictly reciprocal.

Archaeology continues to confirm the consistency with which symmetrical exchange pervaded Greece, particularly during the archaic period. J. N. Coldstream (1983) examined large Attic clay kraters, *skyphoi* and other items with prestige value, which were found as far away from Athens as Tartessos in the eighth century B.C.E., and concluded that these

---

[3] A good review of Polanyi's work and its impact, along with that of Gernet and the contribution of structuralism generally to the social and economic exchange of classical Greece, can be found in Humphreys 1978, 31–75.

were gifts presented in exchange for access to valuable metal routes. Ian Morris (1986b) examines the evidence for the extent to which gift exchange pervaded the Greek world at the time of Homer and argues that its purpose was to establish friendly relations between individuals and households or to normalize social relations that had been disrupted, and to maintain the status gradations in society. Morris contends that the nature of the exchange, which produced an alternating disequilibrium between its participants, preserved the bond between them through a state of alternating indebtedness. Archaeological evidence indicates that this pattern survived the commodity trade that came with tyrants in c. 700 B.C.E., and the subsequent introduction of coinage. Indeed, as Morris points out (1986a), the fundamental imprint that this exchange pattern made on Greek society can account for the general reluctance on the part of Greeks (even at a much later date) to engage in large-scale trading, for this style of commerce ignored the social balance to which the Greeks remained sensitive.

Aristotle cites as the mark of a noble man (*megaloprepês*) not only generosity in using his wealth for the public good, but also the participation in the exchange of gifts (*NE* 4.1123a 4–5). In post-classical Greece the horizontal pattern of reciprocal exchange co-existed with the vertical pattern of *euergesia*, the conferring of benefactions by wealthy individuals or by the now-developed city-state. The mutuality of the horizontal system persisted in the language of the new pattern, even when an equivalent response was impossible. The response of the poor to receiving a gift from a donor (*philanthrôpia*), however modest, was called *philanthrôpon:* The vocabulary preserves an equivalence that is, however, no longer there (Hands 1968, 36). But the obligation among individuals to reciprocate kindness was slow to disappear. Private bonds established by reciprocity persisted along with the public demand to become a benefactor of an entire group—the poor or the state as a whole. Conflicts and misunderstandings arose as two incompatible systems coexisted, and the earlier network of private bonds between reciprocal donors resisted dissolution. A study of this conflict has been made by G. Herman (1987). M. W. Blundell (1989) discusses the ways in which the earlier pattern of reciprocal exchange operated in friendship (*philia*) during the post-classical period, particularly in rhetoric. The language of the orators insisted on the obligation to requite the pleasure-bearing component in friendship, i.e., *charis*. The basis for this persistence is, as she points out, that a relationship between friends is founded on trust, something that makes the individuals vulnerable to treachery and dependent on this protection (34).

L. Kurke has produced a study of Pindar grounded in an appreciation of the cardinal role played by social reciprocity in epinician poetry (1991). Calling it a study in "sociological poetics," she calls upon the pattern of gift-exchange which secured guest-friendship (*xenia*) in the archaic Greek world, to explain much of the imagery in Pindar's verse. Building on M. Mauss' demonstration of the totality of the pattern of reciprocity in societies dominated by the gift-exchange system, Kurke argues that Pindar incorporates this into his poetry, in every step of the epinician process. The victory of the athlete and the celebration of the event with the performance of the praise poem inspire a poetic nexus of reciprocal gifts, cementing bonds between the victor and his community, between the victor and the poet, and between mortals and the gods.

But the reciprocal exchange of goods and favors, although necessary for an understanding of *charis* in archaic Greece, is not sufficient. The poets also described an encounter with beauty, whether in men, women, or in poetry itself, as *charis*. A beloved, a radiant victor in epinician verse or even the poet's words of praise, are experienced as *charis*. As beautiful objects, these all confer pleasure, and this pleasure provokes a response, like the unsettling pleasure produced by a gift or a favor. The language reflects the similarity of these experiences and the form that these experiences took.

As in the exchange between Hypnos and Hera, *charis* designates the process and is applied both to the beautiful object
that arouses a response, and to the response itself.

This bifocal application of the word was not peculiar to
charis. The distinction that we are careful to make between
the subjective and the objective participants in an event
with psychological overtones was not a line drawn by the
early Greeks. The word *aidôs*, for example, meant in the first
instance "reverence," "awe," but it could be applied as
readily to the awe-inspiring source of this feeling as to the
feeling itself. Our application of the compound *good-looking*
is a vestige of this practice: The looking subject has merged
with its object.

If *charis* was grounded in a psychological phenomenon—
the disposition to react when confronted with pleasure of a
personal, social nature—and if it belonged to a social process, it necessarily entailed a feeling that was prolonged,
that was retained over time. It did not denote instant gratification that would be forgotten. Hera will keep her *charis*-
pleasure alive in her memory. But the converse was true
also. If the *charis*-convention was ignored, the memory
would register and retain the full effects of the offense. The
aggrieved party would burn with anger until the situation
was corrected, until reparation for the omission was made.

Social bonds created by *charis* exposed the vulnerability of
the human condition. A *charis*-event, provoked by moral or
aesthetic beauty, was disarming: It broke down the barriers
that confined the self, and it demanded that the beneficiary
reach out to another. If this did not happen, the party who
was responsible for conferring the pleasure was left exposed and vulnerable. This was cause for alarm.

Although it argues strongly for the social nature of *charis*,
The Age of Grace is not a sociological study. It is an attempt to
grasp how the poets from Homer to Bacchylides understood the experience of *charis*, hence how they used it in
their poetry. I conclude with a look at *charis* in the *Oresteia*
and, in an appendix, compare the foregoing with the use of

charis in three plays of Euripides. The way in which the word was used by the dramatists, when sophistic rhetoric had begun to challenge every serious concept and practice of Greek life, provides both a confirmation of, and counterpoint to, the seminal role of *charis* in the earlier poetry.

Chapter Two

THE *CHARIS* OF ACHILLES

οὔτ' ἔμεγ' 'Ατρεΐδην 'Αγαμέμνονα πεισέμεν οἴω
οὔτ' ἄλλους Δαναούς, ἐπεὶ οὐκ ἄρα τις χάρις ἦεν
μάρνασθαι δηΐοισιν ἐπ' ἀνδράσι νωλεμὲς αἰεί.

Nor do I think that Agamemnon son of Atreus nor
the other Danaans will persuade me, since there was no
charis,
then or now, for fighting against enemy-men, ever tirelessly.

Il. 9.315–17

THESE WORDS present the most serious violation of
the *charis*-convention in Greek literature. With Agamemnon's failure to award Achilles the *charis* that
was his due as a superior warrior, the Greeks almost sacrificed their anticipated victory at Troy. Achilles had borne the
brunt of the fighting around Troy prior to the quarrel (*Il.*
1.163–68), but when it came to the apportionment of the
booty by his commander-in-chief, Agamemnon kept for
himself the greater prize, leaving Achilles a paltry portion
(167). At this point, however, the issue is not awards but
amends, amends for which Achilles will hold out.[1]
Agamemnon, anxious to persuade Achilles to reenter the
fighting (because the Greeks were taking heavy losses in the
war without their best fighter), sent an embassy to offer
Achilles the restoration of his concubine Briseis and added
to this a massive indemnity of gifts (*Il.* 9.120–56). But for
some reason this does not satisfy Achilles. Despite the ear-

---

[1] The phrase (οὐκ ἄρα τις χάρις ἦεν, *Il.*9.316) indicates that the lack of
fair compensation is felt as keenly in the present as it was in the past. (See
Denniston 1954, 36: "[ἄρα] with the imperfect especially of εἰμί, denoting
that something which has been, and still is, has only just been realized. In
such cases Greek tends to stress the past, English the present, existence of
the fact.")

nest pleas of his comrades Odysseus, Phoenix, and Ajax, framed in some of the most persuasive rhetoric of the *Iliad*, Achilles holds out. He holds out because, in his view, the offer does not constitute *charis*.

For this he has been condemned by modern scholars, who see him rejecting outright the archaic convention of requital and acting perversely, outside the heroic code.[2] Others are drawn to Achilles by this resolute withdrawal from his group and see in him a proto-tragic figure.[3] Still others see in this a mark of his transcendence of the mortal melee, a sign of his semi-divinity.[4] In antiquity the moral assessment of Achilles' behavior was no less vigorously debated; in fact, it was such a fertile topic of controversy that it became a stock debating subject in the rhetorical schools.

Achilles' lack of *charis*-pleasure was linked to his frustration over not receiving his due recompense. Not only was his small share of booty out of proportion to his contribution to the fighting, but his honor had received a severe, because public, blow when Agamemnon decided to take Briseis from him, announcing this in the most public location, the place of assembly (*Il*.1.184–85). Awards for positive compensation on the Homeric battlefield were material in nature, were carefully calculated, and were seriously affected by the fact that they were conferred in public, in front of other soldiers equally sensitive to honor or shame. An exemplary soldier got his satisfaction in part from receiving his due portion of gold and booty from a raid, but ultimately from his recognition that this reflected a certain amount of prestige, of public approbation (*timê*) from his comrades.

The courageous acts of the Homeric hero were not performed with the sole aim of reaping individual gain but were part of a reciprocal transaction. Heroes brought *charis*

[2] E.g., Sheppard 1922, 69–70; Finley 1978,117; Bowra 1930, 193 ff.; Lloyd-Jones 1983, 26; MacCary 1982, 55–56; Schein 1984, 105.

[3] E.g., Bassett 1934, 62–69; Wade-Gery 1952, 44; Parry 1956, 1–7; Motto and Clark 1969, 120n. 2.

[4] E.g., Jaeger 1945, 420n.27; Eichholz 1953, 144; Whitman 1958, 181–220; Rosner 1976, 314–27; Adkins 1972, 305; Arieti 1985, 193–203.

to their commanders. Not only did the commander feel pleasure after the triumph of a successful skirmish, but this pleasure established a bond between him and his subordinates who helped bring about the victory.[5] What the good commander provided in turn was responsible leadership in battle and the rewarding of his successful subordinates with an appropriate share of the spoils, their *geras*. On both these counts Agamemnon had failed, according to Achilles. He

[5] χάρις, then, is the word we find in the following passages: *Il.* 5.211, describing Pandarus' sacrifice on behalf of Hector (φέρων χάριν Ἕκτορι δίῳ); *Il.* 9.613, Nestor's siding with Agamemnon against his comrade Achilles (Ἀτρείδῃ ἥρωι φέρων χάριν); *Od.* 5.307, of the Greeks in general, who sacrificed their lives for the two leaders of the expedition to Troy (χάριν Ἀτρείδῃσι φέροντες). Like χάριν φέρειν, χαρίζεσθαι is used for the exemplary act of favoring one's comrades and commander in the war, at *Il.* 15.449 and 17.291.

At *Il.* 15.744 we find an instance of χάρις in this context that is particularly interesting, in that it anticipates a later grammatical use of the word. Ajax is attacking whoever of the Trojans makes an attempt to set fire to the Greek ships. This Trojan he describes as ὅς τις δὲ Τρώων κοίλης ἐπὶ νηυσὶ φέροιτο / σὺν πυρὶ κηλείῳ, χάριν Ἕκτορος ὀτρύναντος, "whoever of the Trojans rushes onto the hollow ships with devouring fire, the χάρις of Hector rousing (his troops)." The pleasure of the χάρις belongs of course to Hector, who would be seeing some of his troops respond to his rallying call and succeed in making their way to the Greek ships, but χάριν functions as an accusative in apposition here, or possibly as an adverbial accusative. (See Appendix 2.) Here we can see the foundation for the later use of χάριν as a preposition meaning "for the sake of." At this stage it is practically synonymous with χαριζόμενος, or φέρων χάριν Ἕκτορι δίῳ, *Il.* 5.211 (see Leaf 1886 *ad Il.* 15.744), and retains the significance of the noun χάρις. But the pleasure would not be confined to Hector alone. The bringing of fire to the Greek ships is a χάρις that is bifocal: It contains the anticipated pleasure of the soldiers who would be rewarded later for valiant service, should the Trojan effort succeed. In referring to both subjective and objective pleasure, χάρις reflects the bond and mutual dependence between the commander and his subordinates.

Soldiers regularly hoped for glory and acclaim as appropriate return for exemplary χάρις-service. Pandarus is promised χάρις and κῦδος (glory) if he breaks the truce with the Greeks and lets fly an arrow at Menelaus (*Il.* 4.95). In addition to acclaim, he will receive material compensation from Paris, if he kills the Greek king (97). Here the χάρις of Pandarus refers to something psychological (his pleasure) but also the concrete cause of this, a reward.

had played the coward by letting Achilles do all the fighting (*Il*. 9.322–33), and he had cheated him of his *geras*. Although the ideal was clearly that of symmetry, reciprocity, and mutual dependence, seeds for dissension were sown in the system by the fact that a commander-in-chief could claim a *geras* by virtue of his position, a prize to which a superior soldier had an equally valid right to lay claim.[6] Both would lay claim to the prize because they had calculated that the *timê* it represented was their due. *Timê* is usually translated by "honor" or "prestige," but as "pleasure" is an inadequate translation for *charis*, to cover the various contexts in which the word is found, so "honor" and "prestige" do not give a complete picture of *timê*. *Timê* is possibly linked etymologically with the most important Greek word for compensation, *tisis*, and its congeners like *tinein* (to make amends). This suggests that in the Indo-European matrix from which Greek society sprang there was a process common to both.[7] At *H. Dem*. 123–32, the goddess Demeter tells a story in which she escapes from pirates who hoped to get a ransom, a *timê*, for her. Here the word clearly means "price" and not "honor." It was not the prestige of *timê*, but rather commercial gain that the pirates hoped to obtain by her capture. Frequently, *timê* comes close to the meaning of

[6] The rival claims are reflected in Agamemnon's warning that Achilles should keep in mind that his commander was βασιλεύτερος (more kingly) and therefore merited submission by his subordinates (*Il*. 9.160). Donlan 1982b, 158nn. 37, 38, presents this conflict as the clash of two political models operating simultaneously in the epic, expressing the tensions of a society in transition from the egalitarian to the hierarchical. There is no independent historical evidence for this, however, and the ambiguities could simply have been tolerated within one political system.

[7] Pokorny 1959, I.637, links τῑμή, τίω, and ποινή, deriving them all from *kᵘei- ("respect, punishment, expiation"). Benveniste 1969, II.51, separates τῑμή, τίω (<*kᵘēi) from τίνω, τίσις (<*kᵘēi-). *LSJ* gives three distinct meanings for τιμή: (i) honor (ii) worth, value, price (iii) compensation, satisfaction, penalty. It suggests that this may be accounted for by a contamination from τίνω: Both share the aorist active ἔτισα. But morphologies are not haphazard, and whether the two word-groups are legitimately or falsely linked, there seems to have been a conscious will at some point to allow the two to reflect the basic notion of *due calculation*.

tisis (requital-payment).[8] If Paris is defeated in the duel with Menelaus, the Trojans must return Helen and her gifts and in addition must pay *timê* (*Il.* 3.284–87). They must go beyond simple restitution and pay a price, an indemnity, for the loss in prestige and enjoyment of Helen suffered by Menelaus.[9] *Timê*, then, can have the evaluatively neutral sense of "calculation" or "price," as well as the positive sense of honor or the satisfaction that results from a restitution payment, a *tisis*.

Timê, based on a correct calculation, could also denote one's prerogative. Here once again calculation is involved, the calculation of one's worth. The precocious young Hermes in the Homeric Hymn in his honor is awarded a *timê* from Zeus, his prerogative among the gods (516). He had impressed the Olympians with his cleverness and by his music had converted the anger of Apollo to love (434). Apollo rewards him with the *timê* of presiding over barter-exchanges between people as well as certain kinds of proph-

---

[8] τίσις, the indemnity-payment, involves a calculation of the τιμή (worth) of the aggrieved party. A βασιλεύς could arrange a τίσις for reparations that almost amounted to a levy or tax throughout the community. Telemachus would have the right to issue such a levy, to replace *in toto* the contents of his οἶκος that had been devoured by the suitors, if the supplies had disappeared at the hands of Ithacans (*Od.* 2.78). At *Od.* 22.55–57 the suitors, fearing for their lives at the hands of Odysseus, offer to go throughout the δῆμος and procure a replacement for all that they have eaten and drunk in Odysseus' palace. They calculate the price (τιμή) as the value of twenty oxen apiece. Alcinous also describes such a levy imposed upon the δῆμος, replacing the goods given to Odysseus by the Phaeacian counselors (*Od.* 13.14–15). The verb he uses for "levy" is τίσεσθαι.

The all-important calculation looms large when Agamemnon and Achilles haggle over the indemnity payment for the loss of Chryseis at *Il.* 1.121–87. Achilles offers, on behalf of all the soldiers, to pay back (ἀποτίσο-μεν, 127) three- and four-fold her worth, when the common stores are ample again. Agamemnon is not satisfied with the offer; he wants immediate recompense. Only this is ἀντάξιον (136).

[9] For a fuller discussion of τιμή as reparation-payment, see Vatin 1982, 275–77. In the Greek market today, to ask the price of something is to ask its τιμή. We preserve both the positive and the neutral senses in the modern English doublets that incorporate the τιμή-root, "esteem" and "estimate."

ecy (516–32). To this Zeus adds the privilege of free passage to the underworld and back (572–75). The hymnist describes Hermes' award as the friendship of the reconciled Apollo to which Zeus adds *charis*. (The idea that *charis* represents the "topping up" of something good is one that occurs elsewhere in the poets.) Hermes' activity earned him his *timai* from the gods; these were calculated on the basis of his worth (his *timê*) as a new god. Beyond this, he pleased the gods, and Zeus reacted with a return-*charis*, a favor of particular significance—one that was not granted lightly, even to the gods.

Zeus himself was awarded a *charis* that consisted of the privilege of carrying the thunderbolt. In the *Theogony* we are told that in return for releasing his father's brothers from the fetters in which they had been bound by Cronos, Zeus received the *charis* of the thunderbolt and lightning:

οἵ οἱ ἀπεμνήσαντο χάριν εὐεργεσιάων
δῶκαν δὲ βροντὴν ἠδ᾽ αἰθαλόεντα κεραυνὸν
καὶ στεροπήν·

And they were mindful of him, for his *charis* of kind deeds,
And gave him thunder, the fiery thunderbolt,
And lightning.

Theog. 503–5

This *charis*, the awarding of merited privileges to the gods, is pleasure remembered, resulting in a *charis*-exchange, like that between Hera and Hypnos. It is precisely what Achilles is demanding.

Achilles was angered because Agamemnon had not awarded him his due share of *timê* and indeed had gone further in publicly stripping him of *timê*. Leaning on the sceptre in front of the assembly, Achilles turns to Agamemnon and takes a solemn vow. He will pull out of the fighting, leaving the sons of the Achaeans to die at the hands of manslaughtering Hector (*Il.* 1.239–43). "You will devour your own heart in despair then," he continues, warning Agamemnon, "because to the best of the Achaeans you gave no *timê*" (243–44, cf. 171, 9.648).[10] Later, Achilles will tell the embassy that he withdrew to his tent and could not be persuaded to return because he was given no *charis*. In a culture whose social manoeuverings were largely directed by the awarding of praise or by punishment with its reverse, humiliation, it comes as no surprise that Achilles' *charis*-pleasure could only come from receiving his due portion of *timê*. The awarding of due portions lay behind the archaic Greek notion of justice, *dikê*.[11] For the Greeks the cosmos, like human society, maintained its stability through the equilibrium produced by a balance of opposing forces. If one force or one person encroached upon the allotted por-

[10] Achilles' behavior, far from being perverse and in defiance of the mores of the *Iliad*, was just like that of the gods. The Trojan War itself was fought to compensate for the shame that two goddesses had received at the hands of a Trojan. Hera and Athena make it clear throughout the epic that they will not be satisfied until their τιμή is restored, with the destruction of Troy.

That it is τιμή which Achilles seeks is reinforced in the supplication-scene (*Il.* 1.495–516), where Thetis clasps the knees of Zeus and asks for a return favor from him, that the Trojans gain in strength over the Greeks until τιμή is restored to Achilles. τιμή and its cognates, including the possible cognates from τίσις, occur five times in six verses, underscoring the fact that Thetis requests one thing only:

> Father Zeus, if ever before I was of benefit to you among the
>   immortals
> in word or deed, grant me this wish:
> give *timê* (τίμησον) to my son, who is the most short-lived of all
>   others.
> But even now the king of men Agamemnon deprived
> him of *timê* (ἀτίμησεν). He seized and keeps Achilles' prize, which he
>   personally took from him.
> But do you give him honor (τεῖσον), Olympian counselor Zeus,
> put strength in the Trojans, for as long as it takes the Achaeans to
> honor (τείσωσιν) my son, and until they increase his *timê* (ὀφέλλωσίν
> τέ ἑ τιμῇ).
>
> *Il.* 1.503–10

[11] On this see Palmer 1950, 158–63.

tion of another, restitution had to be made, to restore the equilibrium.[12] Equality, the counterpoise of equals, reflected a healthy community, a harmonious cosmos. Hoping for the restoration of order is a hope that things "will be equal"(e.g., *Od.* 2.203–4). Participating in an "equal feast" was a sign of taking one's place in the orderly, "just" arrangement of heroic society. Achilles withdraws from such a feast, even when he returns to the fighting in *Iliad* 19, because the death of Patroclus has upset the balance, intolerably, until reciprocal action is taken.[13] In *Il.* 9, Odysseus had assured Achilles that he could still participate in the "equal feast" in Agamemnon's tent (266). But in Achilles' view, the feast cannot be equal. The equality has been destroyed by Agamemnon's lack of *charis*, and the return of Briseis, along with indemnity gifts as numerous as the grains of sand or dust (385), would not redress the balance. In some way, Agamemnon has miscalculated the price of reconciliation, the *timê*. His offer does not produce the *charis* of satisfaction in Achilles, the pleasure he might have taken in real requital.

At *Il.* 9.387 we hear what it is that will bring about this satisfaction, the one condition under which Achilles will once again act in solidarity with the Greek forces:

οὐδέ κεν ὥς ἔτι θυμὸν ἐμὸν πείσει ᾿Αγαμέμνων
πρίν γ᾿ ἀπὸ πᾶσαν ἐμοὶ δόμεναι θυμαλγέα λώβην.

---

[12] The best-known testimony for this view is Anaximander's (Anax. 12 B 1 DK). For a discussion of the fragment, see Kahn 1960; Vlastos 1947, 156–78, discusses the cosmic implications of δίκη where it represents "due portion." He illustrates this with an examination of Greek metrical theory and early Greek cosmologies. δίκη involved respecting the nature of the other (i.e., its boundary). Cosmic δίκη involved either (i) repairing the encroachment of one element upon another, or (ii) the successive supremacy of the elements. For other examples of the early Greek view that the balance of opposites composed the lawful regularity of the visible world, see Woodbury 1966, 597–616. For a discussion of Zeus as the protector of τιμή, i. e., retributive, reciprocal justice, see Lloyd 1966, 212–19, and Lloyd-Jones 1983, 6–27.

[13] Motto and Clark consider this but one example of Achilles the "great archetype of honor and fair proportioning" in the *Iliad* (1969, 118–19).

Not even so will Agamemnon persuade my spirit
until he has paid back to me in full that heart-rending
outrage.

Il. 9.386–87

Lôbê (387) is a forceful Greek word meaning "outrage," "mutilation."[14] Achilles had felt the original theft of Briseis as a *lôbê*. When he departed from the assembly deeply angered at his humiliation, he vowed that this would be the last *lôbê* committed against him by Agamemnon (*Il*. 1.232), and that Agamemnon would "tear away at his *thymos*" (1.243) because he had left Achilles bereft of *timê*. The issue at stake is condign retribution. The charged vocabulary at 9.387, "*thymos*-grieving outrage," directly echoes that in Book 1, underscoring the fact that the situation is unchanged, that Achilles still burns with shame and anger. Only when Agamemnon suffers the equivalent amount of crushing humiliation in his *thymos*, deep in the seat of his passions, will Achilles experience the *charis* of satisfaction.[15]

This bald exposé of retributive *charis* demonstrates the degree to which heroic figures were bound together by the

[14] Chantraine 1968 s.v. λώβη: "outrage, violence, mutilation, dit d'une personne qui est un sujet de honte." The Indo-European cognates of λώβη are reserved for heavy stones, weights, etc. See also Arieti 1985, 6.

[15] The fact that Achilles and Agamemnon are locked together by the same λώβη is reflected in the complex and unusual syntax of 9.387: ἀποδόμεναι (to give back, to pay back) takes λώβη as its direct object. Yet Achilles cannot be asking for Agamemnon to return his λώβη; the issue at stake is that Achilles once received this and continues to experience it acutely. We must assign to ἀποδόμεναι here the meaning "to pay back *for*," a meaning not attested elsewhere. It appears to be assimilated to the verb τίνειν, which is found with λώβη at *Il*. 11.142. The giving and taking of λώβη is rooted in one event, and neither Achilles nor Agamemnon will be released from its weight until the injury is paid for in full by the pulverizing humiliation of Agamemnon (Eustath. *ad Il*. 9.386: [ἀπο . . . δομέναι θυμαλγέα λώβην] = ἀντιλωβηθῆναι). This will only happen when the Greek forces are pushed back against their ships by the Trojans, facing certain defeat, and Agamemnon has lost face as a commander. The *charis*-pleasure that arises from satisfaction derived from pain inflicted on another is a paradox favored by the tragedians.

deep gratification that was felt when dues were paid.[16] This was the reverse side of the code which recognized that reciprocal favors initiated a sequence of exchanged kindnesses. The code enjoyed the endorsement of the most basic unwritten law, *themis*, as the aged Laertes reminds Odysseus (in disguise):

δῶρα δ' ἐτώσια ταῦτα χαρίζεο, μυρί' ὀπάζων
εἰ γάρ μιν ζωόν γ' ἐκίχεις 'Ιθάκης ἐνὶ δήμῳ,
τῷ κέν σ' εὖ δώροισιν ἀμειψάμενος ἀπέπεμψε
καὶ ξενίῃ ἀγαθῇ· ἡ γὰρ θέμις, ὅς τις ὑπάρξῃ.

These gifts with which you gave him *charis*-pleasure, extending them in countless number, are for nought.

[16] The view that follows runs counter to that proposed first by Adkins in 1960, 23–32. Since Adkins, scholars have begun to look upon social interaction in the Homeric epics as motivated not primarily by a recognition of interdependence and reciprocity, but by a desire to compete. According to this view, cooperation was of course essential to the heroes of the epic, but it exerted a less powerful influence on behavior than did competition, an agonistic demonstration of ἀρετή. Mary Scott, in a number of articles published recently (e.g., 1983, 1–13), has refined this view with a closer inspection of noncompetitive behavior in the epics. She maintains that the "weaker" gestures like χάρις were examples of enlightened self-interest, expressed only in protected circumstances where there would be no loss of prestige, τιμή. I see in the Achilles example the complete participation of χάρις in the dominant values of ἀρετή and τιμή. (In the case of Achilles, the χάρις he seeks is precisely τιμή.) But I also insist that this was a recognized *collective* convention that, despite the inconsistencies described above, acted as a social, not private (self-interested), check on behavior. Moreover, there were limits imposed upon the rewards for ἀρετή, limits defined ultimately by the cosmic structure and imposed by the social group. These limits dictated that awards be proportional to a performance that would benefit the social group.

Others have questioned the Adkins view. See particularly Long 1970, 121–39, and Dover 1983, 35–48. The Greeks did not resemble ignoble savages like the Cyclopes: Theirs was a society whose conventions were based upon a collective admission of interdependence. The competition for awards, for τιμή, far from being a demonstration of excellence that superseded or defied this admission, was a highly efficient means of ensuring its survival. This finely tuned social mechanism was governed by the calculating Greek mind, which weighed merits and awards, offences and reparations, and insisted on a quantitative parity.

If you had found him alive among the people of Ithaca, he
would have sent you away when he had requited you amply
with gifts in exchange, with kindly hospitality. For it is
basic rightfulness, whenever someone has begun the giving.

Od. 24.283–86

This requital of gifts was an indication that the social order was flourishing, something that was not the case in
Ithaca after the departure of its king. By contrast, the Phaeacians, the idealized society in the epics, demonstrate vitality
and exuberance. Nowhere was this more in evidence than
during the give-and-take of the feast. Odysseus joins them
and sums up the scene of feasting, redolent with *charis*,
where the banqueters enjoy music and the generous sharing of food and drink:

οὐ γὰρ ἐγώ γέ τί φημι τέλος χαριέστερον εἶναι
ἢ ὅτ᾽ ἐϋφροσύνη μὲν ἔχῃ κατὰ δῆμον ἅπαντα
. . . .
τοῦτό τί μοι κάλλιστον ἐνὶ φρεσὶν εἴδεται εἶναι.

I declare that there is no fulfilment more imbued with *charis*
than when joy penetrates everywhere through the
   community
. . . .
This seems to me somehow to be the most beautiful thing
   known in one's understanding.

Od. 9.5–6, 11

The whole experience stimulated total enjoyment (*euphrosynê*), which registered on the senses as well as in the
mind as something very beautiful. The feast was a place to
celebrate community. Often the sharing of communal pleasure was complemented by shared contributions to the meal
(*eranos, Od.* 1.226).[17]

Music was essential to this complete satisfaction at the

---

[17] A recognition of the social bond created by the communal meal
caused the word ἔρανος to be used eventually for other forms of social
obligation. See Hewitt 1927, 160; Donlan 1982, 164; Gerber 1982, 74–75.

Phaeacian feast, but music with certain qualifications. A song should gratify an audience, says King Alcinous: If it cannot bring *charis*-pleasure, it should be stopped (*Od.* 8.538). The words of a Homeric song were vital to its success. Pleasure was to be found in the words, which bore the ethical content of the song (*Od.* 4.239). The words, then, must be ethically appropriate if the audience is to be gratified. In *Od.* 24 we learn that a song about Clytemnestra, who plotted evil for her husband, would be a hateful song (200), but a song about Penelope, who was faithful and mindful only of good things for her husband, will provide *charis*-pleasure (198). It will be a song that will join together mortals and gods, for the gods themselves will stimulate this song among mortals forever. This is an idea developed by the epinician poets, who spoke of songs as *charites*.

Song and dance characterized the famous scene of the Ionian festival on Delos described in the *Homeric Hymn to Apollo*. A spectator coming across the prosperous celebrants honoring the god with competitions in boxing, dancing and song, would say that these people possessed the divine qualities of immortality and perpetual youth. Looking at them, one would "take delight in one's heart, seeing the *charis* of them all" (153). Dancing, competitions, youthfulness, a sense of closeness to the divine, and prosperity represented many of the most prized experiences in the early Greek world. The Ionians' pleasure was of the highest order, and it was infectious. Their *charis* produced delight in the spectator (153).

On social occasions it was important for individuals to be alert to the mutual nature of the experience. In speaking, as Hesiod reminds us, one's tongue must be curtailed, in order not to offend. Otherwise, reciprocal pleasure (*charis*) will become reciprocal discomfort:

γλώσσης τοι θησαυρὸς ἐν ἀνθρώποισιν ἄριστος
φειδωλῆς, πλείστη δὲ χάρις κατὰ μέτρον ἰούσης·
εἰ δὲ κακὸν εἴπῃς, τάχα κ᾿ αὐτὸς μεῖζον ἀκούσαις.
μηδὲ πολυξείνου δαιτὸς δυσπέμφελος εἶναι·
ἐκ κοινοῦ πλείστη τε χάρις δαπάνη τ᾿ ὀλιγίστη.

The greatest treasure among men is found in a tongue that is sparing, and the most *charis* lies in one that conducts itself with moderation. But if you speak ill, quickly will you hear the greater ill spoken of you. Don't be rough at the meal to which many guests are invited. Herein lies the most *charis* and the least outlay amid the common weal.

Op. 719–23

To ensure the greatest personal pleasure, one had to accept the limits on one's "measure" (*metron*, 720)[18] and to keep in mind the pleasure of others. In this the tongue exercised great power: Its ability to please could be abused and with serious consequences. Don't try to please by lying, Hesiod warns:

μηδὲ ψεύδεσθαι γλώσσης χάριν·

Don't lie, with respect to the *charis*-pleasure you give with your tongue.[19]

Op. 709

Similarly, Odysseus rebukes Euryalus for abusing his tongue power in speaking aggressively (*Od.* 8.159–64). Speaking well is one of the *charis*-gifts of the gods (167), like physical beauty or intelligence. A speaker endowed with this gift addresses others with the softening effect that instils awe, *aidôs* (172), and he stands out conspicuous among them: They gaze upon him as if he were a god. Hesiod describes kings who possess such power. When honored and touched by the Muses at birth, they deliver their ordinances with such wisdom and gentleness of speech that they in turn are treated with the same sweet reverence, *aidôs* that comes about through a softening experience (*Theog.* 92). Gentle, appropriate, respectful speech is entirely reciprocal:

---

[18] Both time and place are important in considering the "measure." The scholiast glosses this with advice to measure out the καιρός, the spatial and temporal accuracy of one's tongue. This is a favorite motif of Pindar, who claims for himself just this social and poetic skill.

[19] This translation takes χάριν as an accusative of respect. See Appendix 2.

It delivers and receives a sweet reverence. *Charis* in speech, by stirring pleasure in one's audience, breaks down barriers between people in potentially hostile situations. This is contrasted with disorderly speech, which provokes anger (*Od.* 8.178–79). When the social order breaks down as it does in Hesiod's Age of Iron, *charis* disappears. Virtuous conduct goes without reward:

οὐδέ τις εὐόρκου χάρις ἔσσεται οὐδὲ δικαίου
οὔτ᾽ ἀγαθοῦ, μᾶλλον δὲ κακῶν ῥεκτῆρα καὶ ὕβριν
ἀνέρα τιμήσουσι· δίκη δ᾽ ἐν χερσί, καὶ αἰδώς
οὐκ ἔσται.[20]

Nor will there be *charis* for one who is true to his oath, or just, or good, but rather they will do honor to the doer of evils and the man of arrogance. Justice will be taken into one's hands, and there will be no *aidôs*.

Op. 190–93

Hesiod is placing *charis* once again in the context of *dikê*. Men of good conduct surrounded by the injustice of the Age of Iron do not receive their just rewards, their *timê*. Instead, *timê* is awarded to evildoers (192). This is Achilles' complaint: "In one and the same *timê* are the evildoer and the good man; an equal portion is distributed to all" (*Il.* 9.318–19). The system breaks down when the calculation of appropriate rewards and punishments is inaccurate, therefore "unjust." Sensitivity to others, *aidôs*, disappears and *charis* makes a hasty departure when *dikê* becomes strictly personal and arbitrary, imposed with violence and an attitude that is exclusively self-centred.

This behavior is "ugly," Penelope tells the suitors as they

---

[20] I have opted to retain οὐκ ἔσται instead of adopting West's substitution ἐσσεῖται. West takes αἰδώς and δίκη as parallel subjects of ἐσσεῖται. Although δίκη can conceivably be understood with "violence," αἰδώς and violence are mutually exclusive, and one cannot imagine such a close association in this case. Keeping the standard reading, despite the problems raised by West (1978 *ad loc.*), is, I think, preferable.

consume the livelihood of a king who had treated them with complete fairness (*Od.* 4.686–95). In contrast to Odysseus who had behaved according to the correct pattern (*dikê*) of godlike kings, the suitors displayed no *charis* in return for good works:

ἀλλ' ὁ μὲν ὑμέτερος θυμὸς καὶ ἀεικέα ἔργα
φαίνεται, οὐδέ τις ἔστι χάρις μετόπισθ' εὐεργέων.

But your spirit and your ugly actions show
How there is no *charis* in you after receiving good works.

Od. 4.694–95

Hesiod's Age of Iron, and Odysseus' household without its prince, lack the social lubricant that would protect them from disintegration. Families were microcosms of the society that promoted reciprocal behavior. Children requited kindnesses to parents. If one's child was killed on the battlefield, one would be deprived of this return service, a fact that inspires some of the most poignant tragic reflections in the *Iliad*.[21] We also get an occasional glimpse in the *Iliad* of the most intimate of reciprocal bonds, that between husband and wife. A dying young soldier is described as having "seen no *charis*" from his bride, although he had given a great sum as a bride-price (*Il.* 11.241–42). This of course, as often with *charis*, has sexual overtones but is an explicit reference to the material as well as the erotic interdependence of married partners. The prolonged pattern of mutual benefits, the *charis* between married partners, extends beyond the gratification of desire. The most memorable expression of this in Greek literature is found in Sophocles' *Ajax*. Tecmessa appeals to her husband, on the grounds of their mutually shared *charis*, not to take his life. Ajax, she claimed, was not considering

21 For example, 4.473–79. Thetis, divine mother of Achilles, becomes a prototype of such a parent. She speaks of rearing Achilles like a young plant that is nurtured in an orchard. She will never, however, be able to experience the joy of his returning as a hero from Troy (*Il.* 18.52–62). On the bond between Thetis and her son, see Robbins 1990b, 2.

her needs as he contemplated suicide, and on the grounds of *charis* that begets *charis* she could expect him to be mindful of her:

ἀλλ' ἴσχε κἀμοῦ μνῆστιν· ἀνδρί τοι χρεὼν
μνήμην προσεῖναι, τερπνὸν εἴ τί που πάθοι.
χάρις χάριν γάρ ἐστιν ἡ τίκτουσ' ἀεί·

But keep me in mind too: It is necessary for recollection
to be alive in a husband, if in some way he should experience
joy.
For it is *charis* that is ever the one begetting *charis*.

Sophocles *Ajax*, 520–22

In the *Iliad* the wife of Antenor raised his bastard as her own son, showing *charis* to her husband (5.71). Although mutual gratification was clearly possible in marriage or love relationships in early Greek society, the literary references clearly emphasize the wife's granting favors to her husband.[22] The contribution of the husband is more likely to be seen as that of tutor (e.g., Xen. *Oec.*) or the initial investment of the bride-price. If the pleasures exchanged between partners or comrades were not identical, they were at least symmetrical within the expectations of their culture and a basis from which either member, like Achilles or Agamemnon, could lay claim.

Such a claim was also made by mortals who had offered gifts to the gods. The pattern of *do ut des* ("I give in order that you give") in relation to the gods was certainly not discovered by the Greeks, but the fact that it was based on reciprocal pleasure meant that *charis* was often the word chosen to refer to such an exchange. Mortals gave the gods *charis*-gifts and in return received divine support in battle (*Il.* 8.204) or in personal conflicts (*Il.* 1.39–42). Libations were offered to the gods, so that in their *charis*-enjoyment they would be disposed to make a *charis*-return:"Grant *charis*-filled returns to all the people of Pylos," says Athena (disguised) to Poseidon, after libations have been poured to the god (*Od.*

[22] See Plut. *Amat.* 751, and the discussion of this by Barrett 1964, 433 *ad* 513–15.

3.58–59). Repeating the offerings sustained the bond between mortals and their divine protectors.[23] Poseidon cannot understand why Aeneas should suffer in the war, because he always satisfies the gods with gifts appropriate for a *charis*-bond:

ἀλλὰ τίη νῦν οὗτος ἀναίτιος ἄλγεα πάσχει
μὰψ ἕνεκ' ἀλλοτρίων ἀχέων, κεχαρισμένα δ' αἰεὶ
δῶρα θεοῖσι δίδωσι, τοὶ οὐρανὸν εὐρὺν ἔχουσιν;

But for what reason does this faultless man suffer woes
for no purpose of his own, but because of the sorrows of
others, and he always gives *charis*-bearing
gifts to the gods, who hold the broad heaven?

Il. 20.297–99

Just as between mortals like Achilles and Agamemnon, a violation of the *charis*-exchange between a mortal and a god was cause for concern. Athena upbraids Poseidon for his harsh treatment of Odysseus, on the grounds that the hero had been generous with his sacrifices while at Troy:

οὔ νύ τ' 'Οδυσσεὺς
'Αργείων παρὰ νηυσὶ χαρίζετο ἱερὰ ῥέζων
Τροίη ἐν εὐρείῃ; τί νύ οἱ τόσον ὠδύσαο, Ζεῦ;

Didn't Odysseus give you
charis-favors by the ships of the Argives, making offerings
in broad Troy? Why, then, Zeus, are you now so greatly
vexed at him?

Od. 1.60–62

[23] Often this bond is expressed by χαρίζεσθαι in the perfect tense, denoting "a completed action, the effects of which still continue in the present" (Smyth 1920, 1945). Autolycus repeatedly burned sacrifices pleasing to Hermes (τῷ γὰρ κεχαρισμένα μηρία καῖεν, *Od.* 19.397). As a result the god was favorably disposed (πρόφρων, 398) and bestowed on him the talent for thievery and oaths (396). The same language characterizes the relationship between mortals. Achilles and Briseis reflect their sustained intimacy with Patroclus with the words κεχαρισμένε θυμῷ (*Il.* 11.608=19.287). Sthenelaus, Athena, and Agamemnon appeal to Diomedes with these same words, hoping to make a claim on the basis of their repeatedly proven ties with the warrior. (*Il.* 5.243=5.826=10.234).

Zeus acknowledged the symmetry that held between mortals and gods bonded in this way when he watched the body of Hector being defiled by being dragged around the walls of Troy by Achilles. Zeus was grieved at heart, because Hector had burned for him many thigh-pieces on the peaks of Ida and in Troy (*Il.* 22.169–72). Poseidon uses harsh language to upbraid Apollo for violating this convention of reciprocity (*Il.* 21.441–60). The two gods had helped the founding king of Troy, Laomedon, to build the city walls and herd his cattle. But instead of the reward they expected, they were threatened with violence and chased out of town, furious at the unfulfilled promises. But Apollo seemed to forget the offence: Where he ought to join in the punitive destruction of the insolent descendants of Laomedon, the "witless fool" (441) shows *charis*, as Poseidon observes scornfully:

τοῦ δὴ νῦν λαοῖσι φέρεις χάριν, οὐδὲ μεθ' ἡμέων
πειρᾷ ὥς κε Τρῶες ὑπερφίαλοι ἀπόλωνται
πρόχνυ κακῶς σὺν παισὶ, καὶ αἰδοίης ἀλόχοισι.

But now to his people you bring *charis*, and you don't
make trial with us so that those arrogant Trojans are
destroyed, painfully brought to their knees with their
children and their compliant wives.

Il. 21.458–60

To requite arrogance and insolence with *charis* is folly. But of course two individuals can have conflicting obligations, based on their private loyalties, and what is wisdom to one is folly to another. Zeus' apparent support of the Trojans in the war was due to the claim of Thetis to reciprocal favor (*Il.* 1.503–4), her rightful due ever since she released him from the fetters with which the other Olympians had bound him (*Il.* 1.393–412). But the Trojans' enemy, the Greek king Menelaus, could also expect the protection of Zeus (Zeus *Xenios*), who was obliged to crush the Trojans because of the violation of *xenia*, guest-friendship, by the Trojan who abducted his wife. In the eyes of the Greeks, Zeus' *charis*-

action in favoring the Trojans betrays a startling lack of wisdom (*Il.* 13.633–39). Personal loyalties issuing from reciprocal bonds can result in conflicts of various kinds. They can run counter to the collective, as well as individual, needs. This was discovered in the post-heroic age, as individuals maintained their private guest-bonds even when this conflicted with the needs of the emerging *polis*. The conflict had already surfaced in the *Iliad*. Glaucus and Sarpedon ignored the solidarity with their respective sides in the war, in order to respect such personal family ties of guest-friendship (6.119–236).

Because of the deeply personal nature of *charis-* (like *xenia-*) bonds, the favoring of one partner could easily compete with the needs of another. Ares complains to Zeus that because of the gods' habit of bringing *charis* to mortals they provoke hatred and warfare among themselves (*Il.* 5.873–75). *Charis* created bonds between two individuals by opening them to one another in such a way that each was disposed to act on the other's behalf. Paradoxically, it also created conflict. *Charis* was by nature partisan and active and would naturally generate competing loyalties.

The disarming effect of *charis* is dramatically presented in the divine anointing of Odysseus. The hero, after encountering Nausicaa with her handmaidens on the shores of Scheria, bathes himself and covers himself with the oil and clothing that the young princess provides for him (*Od.* 6.224–37). But the culmination of the effect is produced by Athena. The goddess magnifies his size and strength, curls his locks, and sheds *charis* over his head and shoulders (229–35). Homer compares this to the work of a craftsman trained by Hephaistos or Athena, who overlays gold upon silver, producing works that are *charis*-filled (234). Odysseus sets himself apart from the young woman and sits "glistening with *charis* and beauty" (237). The result of this is that Nausicaa gazes at him in astonishment (237). Now we understand the comparison of Odysseus' unction with overlaying gold upon silver: Human beauty is gilded by divine. *Charis* is more than ordinary beauty; *charis* is gold over silver. This is beauty that moves its beholder to respond. Nausicaa immediately prepares for Odysseus what he most desires, food and drink (246) and the means to enter the city and speak to her father. As king of the Phaeacians, Alcinous can grant the wherewithal for a passage home to Ithaca (289–90).

Athena repeats her transformation of Odysseus when he appears before the assembly of the Phaeacians, where the king will instruct them to prepare a ship for the hero's return to Ithaca. She makes the hero taller and sturdier to behold and covers his head and shoulders with *charis* so that he should appear to them as a friend among strangers (*Od.* 8.21), although at the same time he was "both terrifying and awe-inspiring" (22). These strangers will test him in contests before they will acquiesce in his requests, and for this he needs to appear not hostile, but strong and awesome, disarming.

The goddess Demeter, like Odysseus, is awe-inspiring, possessed of *aidôs* and also *charis* when she enters the house of Metaneira in search of Persephone. In the Homeric Hymn to the goddess, her mortal host greets the unusual guest, commenting upon the *aidôs* and *charis* that are conspicuous upon Demeter's eyes:

Χαῖρε γύναι, ἐπεὶ οὔ σε κακῶν ἄπ' ἔολπα τοκήων
ἔμμεναι ἀλλ' ἀγαθῶν· ἐπί τοι πρέπει ὄμμασιν αἰδὼς
καὶ χάρις, ὡς εἴ πέρ τε θεμιστοπόλων βασιλήων.
ἀλλὰ θεῶν μὲν δῶρα καὶ ἀχνύμενοί περ ἀνάγκῃ
τέτλαμεν ἄνθρωποι· ἐπὶ γὰρ ζυγὸς αὐχένι κεῖται.

Hail, Lady! Since I suspect that you are not born of parents
who are of lowly estate, but noble. *Aidôs* and *charis*
are conspicuous upon your eyes, just as on the eyes of kings
who give out decrees. Yet, though we groan, we mortals
bear the gifts of the gods, of necessity. A yoke is placed on
our neck.

H. Dem. 213–17

Metaneira's words contain an explicit statement of the early Greek belief in a basically feudal relationship that obtained between gods and mortals. The gifts of the gods, the gods' presence among mortals, with the constraints they placed upon them, all these were experienced as a yoke mortals must bear.[24] A feudal relationship is by nature asymmetrical, and based on fear, fear felt by the lesser toward the greater partner. When Demeter had entered Metaneira's house, she had filled the doorway; her head touched the roof, and she filled the entrance with the dazzling light of the divine. *Aidôs*,[25] reverence and fear, had seized the mortal woman as she experienced this epiphany (190). And yet now Metaneira is not paralyzed by her fear; like Odysseus among the Phaeacians, the *aidôs* is tempered by *charis*. *Charis* bridges the great divide between gods and mortals. It is a softening agent, offering relationship, the exchange of kindnesses. Metaneira recognizes this on the eyes of Demeter and immediately invites her inside, offering her all the provisions she can bestow. At the same moment, she requests a reciprocal favor, the nurturing of her late-born son (218–20).

At the end of the *Odyssey*, Odysseus slays the suitors but faces one more trial, and for this he needs to appear impressive. Like Demeter, or like himself earlier among the Phaeacians, he will get what he needs because of his *charis*. The long-abandoned Penelope will not concede readily that the slayer of her suitors is her husband, and she insists on testing his claim to be Odysseus (*Od.* 23.174–80). To prepare for this, Odysseus is bathed and anointed with oil by the nurse, then Athena pours down beauty over his head and shoulders, increases his size, and bathes him with *charis* (156, 157, 162). The objective, although not made explicit by Homer, is to soften up Penelope to accept this man as her husband:

---

[24] The most notable example of this is Agamemnon's assuming the "yoke-strap of necessity" as he prepares to sacrifice his daughter Iphigeneia, responding to the demand of the goddess Artemis (Aesch. *Ag.* 218).

[25] It is important to note that *aidôs* is used here subjectively, of the feeling of Metaneira, whereas at 214 it is the objective *aidôs* that rests on the eyes of Demeter and is the cause of her host's fear.

His heroism in slaying the suitors was not sufficient, and he needs *charis*, gold upon silver. Telemachus also receives a divine unction from Athena when he calls an assembly of Ithacans and the suitors. His *charis*-anointment is intended to raise his stature before his elders, to give him the authority over them which his youthfulness had prevented him from exercising during the absence of his father. The "wondrous *charis*" (*Od.* 2.12) in which the goddess bathes him astonishes the assembly. Like Nausicaa on the beach, the Ithacans marvel at the sight (13). The elders give way, and the first speaker offers the public wish that Zeus may fulfil for him whatever he desires (34). Unlike his father, however, he does not succeed. In the course of his speech, he retreats into an adolescent complaint that he is not up to the task of playing his father's role (58–79). The gifts of the gods are not permanent.

Charis-beauty often performed its charm by dazzling beholders with its sparkle. Nausicaa is captivated by an Odysseus who glistens with *charis*. Penelope uses *aglaïê* (bright splendor), which later became the name of one of the Charites, to refer to her bright beauty as a young wife, beauty she has now lost. The gods destroyed all this bright lustre when Odysseus departed (*Od.* 18.180). Sparkling beauty was erotically attractive to the Greek eye. When Hera dresses for the seduction of Zeus, she fastens on drop-earrings from which much *charis* gleams:

ἐν δ᾽ ἄρα ἕρματα ἧκεν ἐϋτρήτοισι λοβοῖσι
τρίγληνα μορόεντα· χάρις δ᾽ ἀπελάμπετο πολλή.

And into the lobes of her well-pierced ears she put earrings, consisting of three berry-like drops.[26]
And much *charis* gleamed therefrom.

Il. 14.182–83

[26] This follows the interpretation of Kardara 1961, 62–64. μορόεντα has also been translated by "sparkling," understood to be a derivative from the μαρ- root of μαρμαίρω etc. See Leaf 1886 *ad loc*. Several specimens of earrings with triple-drop beads, dating from the seventh/sixth centuries B.C.E., were uncovered by Orsi in Megara Hyblaea (Orsi 1898). These are now in the Orsi Museum in Syracuse, Sicily.

The line is repeated at *Od.* 18.298 to describe earrings given to Penelope by a hopeful suitor. Like the other gifts presented to her by the Ithacans aspiring to her hand, such as robes with gold brooches or gold chains with amber beads "as bright as the sun" (296), the earrings' principal attraction, which accounted for their beauty, was their sparkle. When Athena wants to bewitch the suitors with the beauty of Penelope, she makes her brighter by covering her face with ambrosial beauty, "like the unguent with which Aphrodite anoints herself, whenever she goes to the lovely dance of the Charites" (193–94). Penelope will glisten like Odysseus on the beach, and the effect will be that the suitors like Nausicaa will "gaze in astonishment" (191).

The Greeks loved light and naturally associated it with a positive notion like *charis*.[27] The Charites, attendants of Aphrodite, add lustre to the goddess, washing, anointing and dressing her (*Od.* 8.364–66). In the *Homeric Hymn to Aphrodite* (61–63) they bathe Aphrodite before her encounter with Anchises and anoint her with the lustre found on the immortals. The ambrosial oil is a sparkling that allures.

The luminous *charis* of beauty was irresistible, even for Zeus. An indispensable ingredient in his seduction by Hera is the *charis* that gleams from her earrings, like those of Penelope. This same gleaming beauty is found in Sappho and five times in the ps.-Hesiodic *Catalogue*, where women possess the "sparkle of the Charites."[28] A scholiast on *Argonautica* 3.288, where Medea directs quick darting glances at Jason, describes Medea's sparkling glance toward her beloved as "torches of the eyes." Light and movement are essential to the sparkling glance, and the source of that light is the eyes.[29] Having the sparkle of the Charites, then,

---

[27] The Greek "light-aesthetic" has received considerable attention. See, for example, Mugler 1960, 40–72; Treu 1965, 83–97; Bremer 1976; Fowler 1984, 119–49.

[28] Χαρίτων ἀμαρύγματ᾽ ἔχουσα, Sappho fragments 16, 18, ps.-Hesiod fragments 43.4, 70.38, 73.3, 185.20, 196.6. On this see Brown 1989, 7–15.

[29] The phrase ὀφθαλμῶν ἀμαρυγαί (sparkles of the eyes) is used as a simile for the swift thinking carried out by Hermes in *H. Hermes*, 45. From the scholiast on *Arg.* 3.1018, we get ἀμαρυγάς· τὰς οἷον συνεχεῖς κινήσεις.

meant having the flashing look that was bestowed by the goddesses,[30] a seductive glance. Love, the "limb-loosener," pours out from the eyes of the Charites, according to the account of their birth which is found in the *Theogony*:

τρεῖς δέ οἱ Εὐρυνόμη Χάριτας τέκε καλλιπαρῄους,
'Ὠκεανοῦ κούρη πολυήρατον εἶδος ἔχουσα,
'Αγλαΐην τε καὶ Εὐφροσύνην Θαλίην τ' ἐρατεινήν·
τῶν καὶ ἀπὸ βλεφάρων ἔρος εἴβετο δερκομενάων
λυσιμελής· καλὸν δέ θ' ὑπ' ὀφρύσι δερκιόωνται.

Eurynome bore to him three fair-cheeked Charites,
The daughter of Ocean, possessing a most lovely figure,
Aglaia and Euphrosyne and beautiful Thalia.
From their eyes dripped love as they looked,
limb-loosener; and beautifully did they glance from
beneath their brows.

Theog. 907–11

The love-glance from the eyes is a theme developed by the love poets and is closely associated with *charis* as with the Charites. Aglaia (Radiance) figured prominently in the love-lure and, as the Charites added lustre to Aphrodite to accomplish her erotic purposes, so are they essential to the effective conquest of men by Pandora, the "beautiful evil" sent by Zeus to punish men's insolence (*Theog.* 585). In the story of the creation of Pandora found in the *Works and Days* (60–82), Pandora is fashioned by Hephaistus and adorned with finery by Athena. Aphrodite sheds *charis* over her (60)

From the *Et. Gen.*: ἀμαρύσσω . . . καὶ ἀμάρυγμα καὶ ἀμαρυγάς· τὰς τῶν ὀφθαλμῶν ἐκλάμψεις from Hesychius s.v. ἀμαρύττα· τοὺς ὀφθαλμούς. Movement in general was erotically attractive to the Greeks. Sappho describes the allurement of Helen by her ἔρατον βᾶμα (fr. 16.17). Even the movement of stepping was sometimes described as a flash of light. See, for example, Pindar's *Ol.* 13.36, αἴγλα ποδῶν (gleam of the feet), or *H. Apollo* 202–3, αἴγλη δέ μιν ἀμφιφαεείνει μαρμαρυγαί τε ποδῶν (the gleam and the sparkles of the feet shone round). Bacchylides describes the flash of oiled limbs in the wrestling contest as ἀμάρυγμα πάλας (the sparkle of the wrestling, 9.36).

[30] This takes Χαρίτων as a possessive genitive. See Brown 1989, 11n.17.

and the Charites place a golden necklace on her (73). The object of the whole enterprise is that men should be deceived, swept away by delight at the sight of her (58). The dangerous potential of the love-lure added to Pandora by the Charites was assured by the work of Persuasion (*Peithô*), who directed the natural pleasure in beholding beauty to men's self-destruction. The power of *charis* resides in its unerring ability to provoke a response. Reinforced by persuasion it could be deadly.

The Charites are also present in Hesiod's description of the creation of Pandora in *Theogony* 570–84 (see Fig. 1). In this account, Hephaistus makes for her a headband of gold, "a wonder to behold . . . from which much *charis* breathed" (581, 583).[31] Sparkling clothing was frequently associated with the robing of a beautiful goddess in ancient literature,[32] and it possessed *charis*-attraction. Hephaistus, the god of fine metal handiwork, makes Aglaia, radiant Charis, his wife (*Theog.* 945). In the *Iliad*, this same Charis is described as "she of the glistening headband."[33] Calypso's mantle of

---

[31] For the reading χάρις δ' ἐπὶ πᾶσιν ἄητο see West 1966 *ad* 583. On "breathing" *charis*, cf. the nymph Eurynome (the name assigned to the mother of the Charites at *Theog.* 907), who "breathes" visible beauty out from her eyes (*Cat.* fr. 245.7), or the beauty "breathing" around Demeter, who is bathed in light (*H. Dem.* 276–80). On the synaesthetic importance of breath and light, or breath and emotion, in Greek poetry, see Giacomelli 1980, 140–51.

[32] West 1978 *ad* 73–75, cites Greek parallels for the adornment of goddesses including Aphrodite, or Eastern parallels such as the Sumerian Inanna who, once bathed, anointed, robed, and bejeweled, appears "like the light of the moon." The same luminous beauty appears with Aphrodite in the *Shield of Heracles*. She is πολύχρυσος, "much golden" (8) and, if West's supplement is right at v. 74 of the *Catalogue* fr. 43a, a χαρίεις light breathes from her form, her skin, and her silvery garment. The *Homeric Hymn to Aphrodite* V begins with a call to the Muse to give an account of the works of "much golden Aphrodite" (1), and Sappho appeals to "golden-crowned" Aphrodite (fr. 33.1).

[33] Mycenaean tablets at Pylos show an early connection between *charis* and gleaming metal. The names of bronze-smiths are assembled in the collection Jn 431 (AES). Transcribed by Ventris and Chadwick 1956, 551, they include *ka-ri-se-u* (Khariseus), which, like *ka-ri-si-jo* (Kharisios) is equivalent to the Greek χαρίσιος, and *ka-ro-qo* (Kharoquos or Karoqus), an equiv-

FIGURE 1. *Pandora Attired*, engraving by William Blake after J. Flax-
man. Pandora is shown being adorned by the Charites. A jewel
box lies open at their feet. The Horae, holding fruit and flowers,
look on from the left, and Peitho from the right.

gold and silver is described in the *Odyssey* as "*charis*-filled"
(*charieis* 5.231=10.544). Circe's weaving is also *charieis*, and
is "radiant work" (*Od.* 10.223). But in addition to representing the luminous sparkle of the alluring eyes or adornment,
Aglaia, we are told in the *Theogony*, is the "most youthful of

---

alent to the Greek χαροπός or χάροψ (bright-eyed). Mycenaean names, like
later Greek ones, appear to have been significant, denoting qualities like
brightness, glory, etc. These *charis*-names would have been appropriate for
people working with "gleaming bronze." There appears to have been an
emergency collection of bronze and bronze-workers at Pylos at the time the
tablets were compiled.

the Charites" (945). Particular radiance was associated with young girls and boys at their flourishing prime (their *hôra*), when the attractiveness of the opposite sex, the operation of *charis*, would result in the bearing of children.[34] Thalia, too, contributes to this *hôra* and to marriage, representing that moist freshness of youth that is akin to the moist, swelling buds or young shoots of plants.[35] Hephaistus makes Aglaia his "fresh-blooming," *thalia*-filled wife (*Theog.* 946). Flourishing life is cause for celebration, and *thaliai* is the word used to indicate festivity. Hesiod introduces the Charites as living with the Muses on Olympus amid "festivity" (*thaliai, Theog.* 65). Together, the Muses celebrate the reign of Zeus, when the powers of disorder have been vanquished. Zeus rewards right-loving people who honor *Dikê* with peace, freedom from care, an earth that teems with plenty, flocks and wives that teem with progeny (*Op.* 228–37). They go about their work, like the Charites, in a spirit of festivity (*thaliai*, 231). The Charites and the Muses preside over this well-ordered life that earns fecundity and festivity as its reward. One of the Muses is called "Thaleia" (*Theog.* 77), as one of the Charites was called "Thalia." Peace and good order, hallmarks of the new order, were indications that the

[34] Plutarch explains Sappho's girl without *charis*, her ἄχαρις παῖς (fr. 49) as a girl who has not yet reached the γάμων ὥρα (the *hôra* of marriage, *Amat.* 751d). In a less happy context, it is δώδεκα . . . Τρώων ἀγλαὰ τέκνα (twelve bright children of the Trojans) whom Achilles chooses as the optimal sacrifice on the tomb of Patroclus (*Il.* 18.336–37=23.22–23). These would be young Trojans glistening in their prime.

[35] For the importance of moisture to growth, see Robbins 1968. Robbins describes θαλία and its cogeners such as θαλερός as words that referred to what "wells up, burgeons." The growth takes place primarily through the movement of liquid and is therefore particularly applicable to young things. One is reminded of Odysseus' comparing the nubile Nausicaa to a young shoot (θάλος) that he saw growing on Delos (*Od.* 6.157) or of the young Euryalus reared by Aphrodite among the roses, a θάλος of the Charites (Ibycus, fr. 288). This soft, moist swelling growth dries up with old age (Archilochus, fr. 188) or with sexual wear and tear (Archilochus, fr. 196a).

civil, like the natural, order was at its prime: Peace is described by Hesiod as flourishing, full of *thalia* (*Theog.* 902).

Other daughters born to Zeus immediately after his defeat of the Titans were the Moirae and the Horae. Both of these daughter triads were charged with establishing the confines within which mortals would work and play. The Moirae, of course, distributed good and ill, as they determined the fate of mortals (*Theog.* 906). The Horae, normally associated with the bloom of youthful beauty (the *hôra*) or of the seasons of fruitfulness of the earth, are described as taking care of, setting the seasonal boundaries for, the works of mortals (*Theog.* 903). Of the blessings allotted to mortals, the Moirae could be said to determine the due amount, and the Horae the appropriate time for them, while bearing responsibility for protecting these gifts.

The context within which the Charites are presented for the first time in Greek literature includes festivity, good order, the bestowal of blessings in due measure. But at the basis of it all, as one would expect of *charis*-goddesses, is pleasure and joy, and "Euphrosyne" is appropriately added to the names of "Thalia" and "Aglaia" as the name of one of the Charites. These three aspects can be identified in the cult of the Charites as well as in the literature. Indeed, details about the cult-life clearly informed poets who inserted the Charites or *charis* into their verses, and it is in the interests of understanding these as they presented themselves in the literature that we now turn to look at the divine aspect of *charis*.

Chapter Three

THE CHARITES

Καφισίων ὑδάτων
λαχοῖσαι αἵτε ναίετε καλλίπωλον ἕδραν,
ὦ λιπαρᾶς ἀοίδιμοι βασίλειαι
Χάριτες Ἐρχομενοῦ, παλαιγόνων Μινυᾶν ἐπίσκοποι,
κλῦτ', ἐπεὶ εὔχομαι· σὺν γὰρ ὑμῖν τά < τε > τερπνὰ καί   5
τὰ γλυκέ' ἄνεται πάντα βροτοῖς,
εἰ σοφός, εἰ καλός, εἴ τις ἀγλαὸς ἀνήρ.
οὐδὲ γὰρ θεοὶ σεμνᾶν Χαρίτων ἄτερ
κοιρανέοντι χοροὺς οὔτε δαῖτας· ἀλλὰ πάντων ταμίαι
ἔργων ἐν οὐρανῷ, χρυσότοξον θέμεναι πάρα   10
Πύθιον Ἀπόλλωνα θρόνους,
αἰέναον σέβοντι πατρὸς Ὀλυμπίοιο τιμάν.

<ὦ> πότνι' Ἀγλαΐα
φιλησίμολπέ τ' Εὐφροσύνα, θεῶν κρατίστου
παῖδες, ἐπακοοῖτε νῦν, Θαλία τε   15
ἐρασίμολπε, ἰδοῖσα τόνδε κῶμον ἐπ' εὐμενεῖ τύχᾳ
κοῦφα βιβῶντα· Λυδῷ γὰρ Ἀσώπιχον ἐν τρόπῳ
ἐν μελέταις τ' ἀείδων ἔμολον,
οὕνεκ' Ὀλυμπιόνικος ἁ Μινύεια
σεῦ ἕκατι. μελαντειχέα νῦν δόμον   20
Φερσεφόνας ἔλθ', Ἀχοῖ, πατρὶ κλυτὰν φέροισ' ἀγγελίαν,
Κλεόδαμον ὄφρ' ἰδοῖσ' υἱὸν εἴπῃς, ὅτι οἱ νέαν
κόλποις παρ' εὐδόξοις Πίσας
ἐστεφάνωσε κυδίμων ἀέθλων πτεροῖσι χαίταν.

You who are tutelary heirs of the waters of the Cephisus
and who dwell in an abode with fair horses,
O queens famous in song, Charites, overseers of sleek-rich
Orchomenus, guardians over the Minyans born of old,
listen, when I pray. For with you all things delightful   5
and sweet are brought to fulfilment for mortals,

if a man be skilled, handsome, splendid with renown.
For not even the gods arrange dances or feasts
without the revered Charites. They are stewards
of all things done in heaven, placing their thrones   10
beside Pythian Apollo of the golden bow,
paying homage to the ever-flowing honor of the Olympian
father.

O Queen Aglaia
and Euphrosyne, lover of the dance-song, daughters of the
mightiest of the gods, may you hearken to me now. Thalia, 15
enamored of the dance-song, look upon this festive band
lightly stepping, with propitious fortune,
for with a Lydian melody have I come
singing of Asopichus in carefully practiced verse;
because of you the Minyan house was victorious at Olympia.
                                                            20
Now, Echo, go to the black-walled house of Persephone
bringing tidings of fame to his father,
so that when you have seen Kleodamus you may tell him
that his young son in the glorious hollows of Pisa
has garlanded his locks with winged wreaths from
glorious contests.

                                                 Pindar *Ol.* 14

PINDAR composed the *Fourteenth Olympian* Ode to celebrate the victory of a young athlete from Orchomenus. Orchomenus was the place where the cult of the Charites was believed to have originated, and the victory celebration for which this song was composed involved a procession to their temple. Containing as it does an invocation and enumeration of the gifts of the Charites, the song resembles a cult hymn more than it does an epinician ode; Pindar's words reflect a familiarity with the fundamental religious and social dimensions of this cult, deeply rooted as it was in his native Boeotian soil. For this reason, *Olympian* 14 provides a convenient starting-point for looking at the ways in which the Charites were worshiped, both in Orchomenus and elsewhere in Greece. Variants appear, of course, in the cult as it is found in different places and at different times, but the essential elements are embedded in this song.[1]

You who are tutelary heirs of the waters of the Cephisus
and who dwell in an abode with fair horses,
O queens famous in song, Charites, overseers of sleek-rich
Orchomenus, guardians over the Minyans born of old (1–4)

The ode was probably sung in front of the sanctuary by the river Cephisus where the goddesses first made their appearance during the Bronze Age (Hesiod, fr. 71). From Pausanias we learn that the Charites were believed to have arrived on earth as aeroliths, rocks that fell at the feet of the legendary king of Orchomenus, Eteocles (9.35.1–3; 9.38.1). These rocks were in some way associated with water and with the fertile prosperity of the city, as were other aniconic rocks worshiped in centers not far from Orchomenus.[2] As protecting goddesses of the Cephisian waters, the Charites were bound up with the water-based prosperity of Orchomenus. The wealth of the city was proverbial. Homer compares the gold and treasures flowing into Orchomenus at the time of the Trojan War with those of Egyptian Thebes (*Il.* 9.381). The treasury of King Minyas, excavated by Schliemann (1881), was one of the marvels of the world, according to Pausanias. King Minyas is described by Pausanias as having such large revenues that "he exceeded in wealth all men before him" (9.36.5–6). The Charites, overseers of these Minyans and of sleek-rich Orchomenus, had their own links with water, which in some way pro-

---

[1] The examination that follows is a highly selective commentary on *Olympian* 14. For a more complete analysis, see Verdenius 1987, 103–26.

[2] One of these was worshiped as the Boeotian Heracles *Hyettos* (Rain-bringer); in addition there was the λίθος ἀργός (shining rock) in Thespiai, the oldest aniconic image of Eros (Paus. 9.27; see Nilsson 1955, I, 201–2). The veneration of stones persisted until quite late: Pindar himself is said to have founded a shrine to the mother of the gods when a stone image of her fell at his feet (schol. *Pyth.* 3.137b Dr.).

duced this wealth. The Charites were identified as water-
nymphs (Hes. *Astron.* 291) and were connected with
springs (Callim. fr. 740, Servius *ad Aen.* 1.720, Plut. *Mor.*
301a–c).

The ancient city of Orchomenus occupied the slope of a
steep hill, and the Cephisus wound around the southern
base of this hill in serpentine fashion, feeding Lake Copais.
Archaeological evidence has revealed that during the
Bronze Age, at the time the cult to the Charites was
founded, man-made as well as natural subterranean chan-
nels drained Lake Copais, transforming it into a marshy
plain rich with fish and waterfowl.[3] In classical times the
mere of Copais continued to furnish wealth for Orchomenians, becuase it was filled with large quantities of fish and
waterfowl, eels and reeds for the Athenian market, as we
learn from Aristophanes and Pliny.[4] The Charites were
overseers of this abundance and received gifts from the
grateful inhabitants (Ephorus *FGrH* 70.152).

Listen, when I pray. For with you all things delightful
and sweet are brought to fulfilment for mortals,
if a man be skilled, handsome, splendid with renown.   (5–7)

Among the "sweet delights" conferred by the Charites in
cult and in literature was that of the love bond between men
and women. As *gaméliai* (wedding deities), the Charites presided over marriages of the Athenian young at a festival
called the Apatouria. Here they received sacrifices from the
citizens on behalf of the youths who were being enrolled as

---

[3] For more information on these drains, arising out of current archaeological investigations, see Knauss 1990. A bibliography of other studies of
the drains is found in Rocchi 1979, 10nn58, 59. The drainage works were
undertaken in the Middle and Late Helladic periods. Homer describes a
wealthy Greek warrior from this region who joined the expedition to Troy.
Oresbius lived at Hyle on the slopes above this Cephisian marsh and was,
like the Orchomenians, "strongly intent upon his wealth, in possession of
a very rich district" (*Il.* 5.707–10).

[4] *Acharn.* 872–76, *Pax* 1003–4, Pliny, *NH* 16.66.168–72.

ephebes (young members of the citizenry) and on behalf of those about to marry.[5] We see the Charites on the François Vase, attendants at the wedding of Peleus and Thetis, and they were prominent guests at another important wedding, that of Cadmus and Harmonia (Theognis 15–16). They may have played a role at the sacred marriage of Zeus and Hera, celebrated in the month Gamelion, at a festival that honored young bridal couples.[6] Their blessings at the time of marriage assured that the sexual bond would be an active one: In literature as in cult, the Charites were associated with Aphrodite and Eros.[7] When the accent was on conferring harmony and concord, they were associated with Peitho.[8] Charis, says Pindar, dwells with Peitho in the beguiling beloved (Pindar, fr.123.4).

Among the other sweet gifts for which the Charites were worshiped was the gift of healing. Pindar, in an ode for the ailing Hieron, speaks of the *charis* of "golden health" (*Pyth.* 3.73). At Epidaurus the Charites were found with Asclepius on votive reliefs.[9] Human health is a natural extension of the health of vegetation, and these Epidaurian Charites, one of whom was named Auxesia (Growth), were credited with restoring crops that had been failing (Hdt. 5.82).

revered Charites   (8)

The epithet *semnai* (revered, awe-inspiring), which is ap-

---

[5] (*Et. Mag.* s.v. ΓΑΜΗΛΙΑ). Aphrodite and Hera shared the cult title *Gamêlia* with the Charites, and young devotees of Helen at Therapne signaled their readiness for marriage by cult activities similar to those practiced in the worship of the Charites and Aphrodite *Gamêlia*. See Calame 1977, I, 401.

[6] Schwarzenberg 1966, 21n.18.

[7] In the *Homeric Hymn to Aphrodite V*, they bathe and anoint the love goddess (61), and Sappho describes them conducting Aphrodite and her chorus of Erotes to the bridal chamber (fr. 194).

[8] Fernandes 1962, 97n.99, and Bell 1984, 12.

[9] Jakob Escher gives some examples in his entry in *RE* 3.2158 s.v. *Charites*. At Euboea a funerary inscription implores their protection along with that of Hygieia and the Erinyes (*SIG* 3.1240,21,26).

plied to the Charites elsewhere in Greek literature,[10] suggests that the goddesses had considerable power. As vegetation goddesses and nymphs, they would possess chthonic powers, of which *semnai* is an echo here. In the *Oedipus Coloneus*, Sophocles refers to the power of the dead hero Oedipus as a chthonic *charis* (1752). Iconographic evidence from the archaic period suggests links between the Charites and deities like Hermes or Persephone.[11] As attendants of Persephone, they accompanied the goddess when she left the underworld, performing circle dances (*Orphic Hymn* 43.7–8). In Arcadia, Pausanias tells us, the Charites represented the bright side of dark powers. They were connected with the curing of Orestes from the madness that he suffered because of his bloodguilt. This took place after his sacrifice to underworld goddesses, the Maniae (Madnesses, another version of the Erinyes), who appeared to Orestes dressed in black until he made the appropriate sacrifice, when they appeared to him in white. Pausanias gives us the detail that it was customary to sacrifice to the Charites in this

---

[10] Pindar uses the word to describe the Charites elsewhere, at *Pae.* 3.2, fr. 95.4 and possibly in a restored text, fr. 3.2. In Euripides' *Helen* the σεμναὶ Χάριτες are sent to the grieving Demeter, to alleviate her mourning (1341–44). σεμναί was the traditional epithet of the Erinyes in tragedy, e.g., Soph. *Ajax* 837, *OC* 90, 458.

[11] A relief from the Lycian Harpy-monument (early fifth century B.C.E.) shows three maidens walking toward Persephone, presenting her with a pomegranate, a flower, and eggs; and on a Locrian *pinax* three maidens (Charites?) bring Persephone articles for her toilet. On a relief from Thasos (ca. 480 B.C.E.), three maidens, carrying flowers and a perfume vase, seem about to crown Hermes. A bas-relief from the Athenian Acropolis dating from the late Archaic period shows Hermes leading three dancing women, thought to be the Charites, and a youth (who may represent the donor of the relief). See Lechat 1889, 467–76. The Charites shared with Hermes a sacrificial offering at Eleusis (Roberts 1887, 89–90). We cannot, of course, be certain that the three maiden figures in archaic iconography were Charites. Triads of "maidens" (*korai*) such as the Moirae, the Horae, the Erinyes, and the Eumenides, as well as the Charites, were at this stage overlapping in function and are difficult to distinguish. See Harrison 1912, 192; Farnell 1909, V 430.

place at the same time as to these white goddesses, to whom he refers as "Eumenides" (8.34.1–3).

> *For not even the gods arrange dances or feasts*
> *without the revered Charites.*   (8–9)

Dancing was a regular feature of celebrations in Orchomenus that honored the Charites, right down through the Hellenistic period. At the festival known as the Charisia, participants danced all night and were awarded honey cakes (Eustath. *ad Il.* 18.194). Euphorion mentions dancing at Orchomenus (Pollux 4.95), and we have epigraphic evidence from the first century B.C.E. for the Charitesia at Orchomenus, a pan-Hellenic musical and dramatic festival.[12] Dance was, of course, an integral part of fertility cults, where rhythmic movements invoked divine powers and performed mimetic magic that would stimulate natural and human fertility.[13] Dance was, therefore, a vital part of agrarian festivals, initiation rituals, and weddings, occasions where we might expect the Charites to take part.[14] *Olympian* 14 was itself sung along with a rhythmic dance-step (17). The ritual dance served as a form of *paideia* (cultural and moral instruction) among the Greeks, informing the young through worship.[15] As these young men and women awakened to their own fertility, they danced to arouse the fertility of the earth with leaps, whirling, and gestures that signified their own joy. Plato reminds us of the natural desire of youths to move their bodies in a dance form as an expression of joy (*Laws* 2.653d–e, 672d, 673d). Joy (*euphrosynê*) and

[12] Tod 1954, 159–162; Schachter 1981, 142; and Buckler 1984, 49–53.

[13] See Lawler 1964, 13, 45; Burkert 1985, 102–3, 219.

[14] In the *Geoponica* (11.4), the tradition is preserved that the Charites, daughters of King Eteocles of Orchomenus, were once cypresses who danced. Latte 1913, 72, argues that these Charites are the water-linked divinities who first received the honor of ritual from King Eteocles, a ritual that included the dance.

[15] See Burkert 1985, 147, 219.

youth flourishing (*thalia*) belong with the dance, and Pindar addresses the two Charites who bear these names as "loving the dance-song" (14) and "enamored of the dance-song" (16). We will not be surprised to discover the Charites and *charis* flourishing in the rhythms of epinician poetry that stimulated a dance of celebration, where young life tested itself in the games.

placing their thrones
beside Pythian Apollo of the golden bow (10–11)

Apollo comes to Delphi in the springtime, and with his arrival the earth teems with new life. The god dances and plays his lyre, while the Charites dance around him with the Horaie, Harmonia, Hebe, and Aphrodite (*H. Apollo* 194–96). Pindar describes the Charites as enthroned on Olympus beside Pythian Apollo with his bow. On Delos excavators have found an archaic statue of Apollo containing the three Charites in his hand, which corresponds to a statue described by Pausanias (2.32.5, 9.35.3) and ps.-Plutarch (*de Mus.* 14).[16] Macrobius assumed that the Charites were held in the god's right hand because Apollo was quicker to do good than harm, for it was in his left hand that he held the bow.[17] As the Charites were associated with the Eumenides in Arcadia at the point when Orestes was healed, so this statue identifies them with the god's good gifts that were the counterpart of suffering.[18]

But they are stewards
of all things done in heaven (9–10)

[16] Pfeiffer 1952, 21, dates the statue to between 650 and 550 B.C.E.

[17] *Saturn.* I.17.13, cf. Philo, *On the embassy to the emperor Gaius*, 95. Ps.-Plutarch, perhaps in error, describes the Charites as being in Apollo's left hand. On this see Pfeiffer 1952, 21.

[18] Apollo represented this dual aspect in himself, a god of healing as well as of retribution. For the importance of Apollo in the healing of disorders, of a sociopolitical as well as a personal nature, see Groffridi 1983, 331–36.

Although Pindar does not specify what these Olympian activities are, which are dispensed by the Charites, we may assume that they represent the dances and feasts of the gods or perhaps also the kindly works performed by the gods on behalf of mortals.

During the classical period the Charites came to be venerated and worshiped conjointly with other divinities, and, like the gods whose companions they were, they were celebrated for the benefits they brought to family and civic life. In the Old Market in Athens, they shared cult honors with Peitho (Persuasion) and Aphrodite *Pandêmos* (for all the people) and were worshiped as overseers of concord, peace, and happy marriages.[19] When Athens was liberated from Macedonian rule toward the end of the third century B.C.E., the Athenians dedicated a sanctuary to *Dêmos* (the people) and the Charites, where the generosity and reciprocal deeds (*charites*) of Athenian citizens were celebrated.[20] Benefactions and gratitude for them became increasingly important in this cult of the Charites. In 122 B.C.E. the priest of the *Dêmos* and the Charites became priest of the new benefactor, Rome, and during the Roman Empire the Charites represented the gratitude of the *dêmos* to the emperor.

It was gratitude and reciprocity that became the hallmark of the Charites in the minds of the philosophers of the fourth and third centuries B.C.E. This is particularly clear in Stoic reflections upon the iconography of the three Charites which became popular during the Hellenistic period, and which was frequently copied by Roman, then Renaissance, artists. This image consisted of three female figures dancing in a circle, arms entwined, gifts in hand (see fig. 2). The Stoic

---

[19] Like the Charites, Peitho moved from the milieu of erotic persuasiveness to the more general sociopolitical sphere and like them shared a cult with Aphrodite Pandêmos (see Buxton 1982, 33–34). In the fourth century, πανδῆμος χάρις came to mean "general favor" (Arist. *Rhet.* 1406a26).

[20] *SIG* 227: ὁ δῆμος καὶ ἡ βουλὴ ἐπίσταται χάριτας ἀποδιδόναι (The people and the council know how to give back *charites*). Oliver 1960,106, argues that the Athenian cult of the Dêmos and the Graces stood for the various manifestations of civil concord.

SIC ROM CARITES NIVEO EX
MARMORE SCVLP

FIGURE 2. *The Three Graces*, engraving by Marco Dente. The god-desses are shown disrobed, in the canonical circular formation, arms entwined and holding fruit and flowers. Water flows from urns on either side.

interpretation of this was that the Charites personified re-ciprocal *charis*. The idea, credited to Chrysippus, is largely preserved in Seneca's *de Beneficiis* (1.3.2–10).[21] The Charites' entwined arms represented an unbroken chain of good deeds that return upon the donor. The eldest, most digni-fied, was the donor; the others represented the grateful recipient and the return-giver. All three were young, be-cause good deeds, ever recalled and renewed, never grow old. All three were maidens, as gifts must never be spoiled or corrupted. They were unclothed, so as to be uninhibited in their giving and receiving.[22] This dance was the incarna-tion of *beneficia* (kindnesses) for the Stoics: The goddesses in distributing *charis* personified good deeds freely given, re-ceived, and returned.

O Queen Aglaia (13)

Pindar names Aglaia first of the three Charites and ad-dresses her with the distinguishing title *Potnia* (Mistress, Queen). The radiant aspect of the Charites represented by Aglaia was predominant in their names in Laconia. Here they were only two, *Clêto* (Glorious One) and *Phaenna* (Shin-ing One).[23] Lacedaemon, the founder of Sparta, gave the Laconian Charites their names, according to Pausanias, names that Pausanias finds appropriate (9.35.1). Their gift to Laconia, which brought the people fame and radiance, was probably connected with the draining of water in a manner not unlike the project at Orchomenus. Lacedaemon

[21] Chrysippus may have been drawing symbolic references from a painting by Polygnotus on the walls of the Stoa. See Schwarzenberg 1966, 67–70.

[22] The Charites are nude in the dance described by Euphorion (Pollux 4.95).

[23] Alcman, fr. 62 Calame (quoted in Paus. 3.18.6), cf. Paus. 9.35.1, Athen. 4.139, schol. Eur. *Or.* 626. The names and number of the Charites vary in different cult-centers. Hesiod was the first to give them the three names that became canonical. The fact that Pindar follows him in this is likely a reflection of the dominance of the Boeotian cult.

established their sanctuary by the river Tiasa, who was said to be a daughter of Eurotas (Paus. 3.18.6; 9.35.1). Eurotas, also the father-in-law of Lacedaemon, actually created the river that bore his name, by draining the stagnant water that had accumulated on the plain after a flood, and by leading the water through a trench to the sea (Paus. 3.1.1, schol. Eur. *Or.* 626).[24] As in sleek-rich Orchomenus, the draining of the plain probably resulted in brilliant prosperity, vegetation in a fertile ground.

Antimachus connected the Charites with light, describing them as "daughters of Helios and Aigle" (fr. 95W). Hesychius glosses this genealogy with the explanation "because the Charites ought to be bright, radiant."[25] Linguistic equivalents of *charis* and the Charites in other Indo-European languages possess as their primary meaning "light" (not "pleasure"), and as a result scholars have been led to make similar claims on behalf of the Greek words.[26] The association between experiencing joy and feeling radiant is a common one. The English language reflects this, for example, in the expression "beaming with joy." The original meaning of our word *glad* was "bright" (cf. William Blake's "Glad Day"). We have even distorted the correct form of *delite* (< *delectare*, to "delight"), inserting the element of illumination that goes with rejoicing.

---

[24] The mother of this hydraulic engineer-king Eurotas was called Kleochareia, a name that contains within it the ("fame") root *kle-* and the *char-* root of the word *Charites*. Eurotas also married "Kleta," the name Lacedaemon awarded to one of the Charites.

[25] S.v. Αἴγλης χάριτες.

[26] See, for example, Haggerty Krappe 1932, 155–62. For a discussion of this and other claims made for the connection between the Charites, *charis*, and light, see Borgeaud and MacLachlan 1985, 5–14. Light, like reciprocity, dominates the conceptual and social configuration of Greek life generally, especially during the archaic period. Representing experiences of the highest order, these are two phenomena in which *charis* and the Charites participate. This is distinct from making the claim that either of these concepts constitutes the basic meaning of *charis* or the Charites. Rather, we can expect light or reciprocity to appear in literary or ritual contexts where *charis* and the Charites occur.

As is clear from Homeric texts, bright things were attractive to the Greeks. Not only did they describe human beauty as sparkling, but the epiphanies of their gods and goddesses took place in dazzling light. Light marked a state of blessedness. When Demeter enters the house of Metaneira, she sheds the guise of an old woman; around her "beauty emanates" and "the whole house is filled with lightning brilliance" (*H. Dem.* 278–80). Mortals who are singled out for special favor are bathed in light, like Diomedes or Achilles on the battlefield who, when Athena comes to their aid like a burning fire or a star, are said to flame like beacon fires (*Il.* 5.1–8, 18.207–14). Light bound a benevolent god and a radiant mortal together. As Diomedes flashes with fire, demonstrating the assistance of Athena (*Il.* 5.7), a victorious athlete is "set on fire" by the Charites (Pind. *Pyth.* 5.45). Orchomenus can shine because of Potnia Aglaia.

> *Euphrosyne, lover of the dance-song and Thalia,*
> *enamored of the dance-song, look upon this festive band*
> *lightly stepping, with propitious fortune.* (15–17)

Euphrosyne (Joy, Merriment), the second of the Charites to be mentioned, characterizes the feeling that wells up in the group of celebrants as they dance in honor of the young Asopichus. Thalia is asked to bless the procession. The goddess, representative of burgeoning life, is an appropriate patron of the young. Aglaia would be mistress of the event as well, not only because of the glory and fame generated by the victory that the *kômos* celebrated (21, 24), but also for the radiance of youth at its prime. In Laconia the radiant Charites were worshiped in the vicinity of places of particular importance to the young. Near their sanctuary set up by Lacedaemon was a shrine of Artemis *Korythalia* (of flourishing young manhood), where nurses brought young boys during the Titthenidia ("Nurse-Festival," Athen. 4.139 a–b). Near the Spartan racetrack was another sanctuary of the Charites (Paus. 3.14.6). In Athens, the Charites (along with other divinities) were invoked by young men when they took the oath upon being admitted into the administration of the *polis*. This was a rite of passage which in earlier times might have consisted of physical contests.[27] The Charites invoked for the oath are called Thallo (Flourishing), Auxo (Growth), and Hegemone (Guide). The names of the first two indicate that the goddesses presided over youth; Hegemone would be invoked to ensure safe conduct.[28]

In *Olympian* 14 the blessing of the *kômos* celebrating Asopichus will come about when Thalia looks upon him with favor. The Charites had traditionally looked upon Orchomenus in this way; they were its overseers (4). A number of divinities who appear in Greek literature had the power to turn a benevolent gaze upon the world. Helios nourishes things with his look (Eur. *Hipp.* 1279–80) and is associated with fair fortune (*Ol.* 1.5, 13.37). Callimachus appeals to the benevolent look of Artemis which makes things flourish (*Hymn to Artemis*, 129–31).[29]

Now, Echo, go to the black-walled house of Persephone
bringing tidings of fame to his father. (20–21)

But the bright, joyful aspect of the Charites takes meaning from its opposite, as the Eumenides/Charites take on significance by contrast to the Erinyes. The radiant celebration of

---

[27] The oath is preserved in an inscription published by Robert 1938, 297. On the connection with physical contests, see Rocchi 1980, 19.

[28] She would conduct the young through puberty. τὰ ἡγεμόσυνα were rites of sacrifice offered in gratitude for safe conduct. Artemis Hegemone, like the Charites, had a sanctuary near the Spartan racecourse (Paus. 3.14.6). The variation in the names and number of the Charites and their overlap with the function of the Horae, Muses, nymphs, etc., testifies to their original associations with the same powers. Pausanias, for example, at 9.35.2–3, describes the Athenian Charites as two, Auxo and Hegemone, but mentions that there was also an Athenian mystery-cult of three Charites, who were worshiped at the entrance to the Acropolis. He says that the Athenians worshiped the Horae as Karpo (Fruitfulness) and Thallo.

[29] W. Deonna 1965, 149–50, cites Egyptian parallels for *l'oeil créateur* (the creating eye) that creates light, the world, heaven, earth, vegetation, animals, and people.

Olympian 14 is taken to the "black-walled" house in the underworld by Echo, where it can be shared by the young victor's deceased father. The poem ends where it began, with the *charis* that continues beyond the grave, because, since the days of the Minyans of old, the gifts of the Charites are ultimately divine.

Chapter Four

EROTIC *CHARIS*

ἀλλ' ἐγὼ τᾶς ἕκατι κηρὸς ὣς δαχθεὶς ἕλᾳ   10
ἱρᾶν μελισσᾶν τάκομαι, εὖτ' ἂν ἴδω
παίδων νεόγυιον ἐς ἥβαν·
ἐν δ' ἄρα καὶ Τενέδῳ
Πειθώ τ' ἔναιεν καὶ Χάρις
υἱὸν Ἁγησίλα.

But I, on (Aphrodite's) account melt like the wax
Of sacred bees pricked by the stinging heat of the sun,
Whenever I look upon the fresh-limbed youthfulness of boys.
Right in Tenedos, you see,
Peitho and Charis reside
In the son of Hagesilas.

Pindar fr. 123.10–15

NOW it is a young beloved, rather than an athlete, who is receiving the attention of Pindar. We are told by several sources that Theoxenus was a young man loved by the poet and was present at Pindar's death.[1] It is the *hêbê* (youthfulness) of Theoxenus that Pindar finds irresistible: The *hêbê* accounts for the powers of Charis and Peitho. Theoxenus was on the threshold of manhood, the point when youths became attractive to lovers in

---

[1] For this evidence see van Groningen 1960, 76–77. His chapter 5 (51–83) consists of a useful commentary on this eulogy. Van Groningen would alter the χάρις of 12 to χάρισ', to avoid the difficulty introduced by ἔναιεν with a direct accusative (υἱόν) as well as the prepositional phrase ἐν . . . Τενέδῳ. The verb χάρισ' predicates of Peitho: "Apparement Peitho habitait à Tenedos et y a fait le gracieux cadeau du fils d'Hagésilas" (72). I know of no other contexts where Peitho *makes* a gift rather than residing in one (cf. Pandora), and the common partnership of Peitho and Charis—as divinities, powers, or qualities—suggests χάρις should be kept. For ναίω followed by a direct object, see *LSJ* s.v. ναίω I 1b.

Greek society.[2] Pindar elsewhere describes a boy at this stage as "beautiful in his form, blended in his *hôra* (his ripening manhood)," like Ganymede (*Ol.* 10.103–4). At the *hêbê* or the *hôra*, the awkward elements of the ungainly adolescent blended into a harmonious whole. This was the moment when young men and women would be, like Ganymede, approached by a lover.[3]

Pandora, like Theoxenus, received her powers of enticement from the Charites and Peitho (Hesiod, *Op.* 73). She was a young woman at her *hôra*: Horae garlanded her with spring flowers (75). The Horae were forces of nature, the seasons brought to fruitfulness. Young men and women at their *hôra* had reached the moment when they were ripe for love, and they were frequently described like Pandora— garlanded, or picking flowers.[4] Athenaeus preserves some words of Clearchus of Soli on this subject, taken from his *Amatoria*. People, he says, have a fondness for carrying fruits and flowers because of their attraction to the *hôra*. "Beautiful is the look of the ripening of fruits and flowers," he continues, "and it is natural to speak of those whom one thinks of as beautiful and at their *hôra* as picking flowers"(fr. 25 Wehrli). Hence, the rape of Persephone occurs when she and her young handmaidens are picking flowers (*H. Dem.* 5–6). Sappho describes the image of a very tender young girl

---

[2] Pindar mentions the "young limbs" (10); other features that defined this moment included the beard that would be in evidence but not fully grown (Plato, of Alcibiades, in *Protagoras* 309a; Dover 1978, 85–86).

[3] For the importance of a proper "mixing" of the elements at the *hôra*, cf. Plato, *Symp.* 188. We can recognize this moment, but it is significant that we have no word for the *hôra*, perhaps because in our culture the event is less significant; the young at this age are not candidates for erotic attachments with an older male or female.

[4] In the *Cypria* (4) Aphrodite is clothed in garments made for her by the Charites and the Horae, robes tinted with the dye from spring flowers (crocuses, hyacinths, violets, roses, lilies, narcissi). These, the poet tells us, are the flowers worn by the Horae, and Aphrodite with the Charites and nymphs crown themselves with garlands of these flowers as they sing on Mount Ida. For the role of flowers in the iconography of abduction scenes found in Greek vase-painting, see Sourvinou-Inwood 1987, 137.

picking flowers (fr. 122) and frequently associates flowers and flowery garlands with young girls' experiences of love (e.g., frs 81, 94, 96, 98, 105). From pseudo-Galen we get an explanation of this association: The origin is pleasure, pleasure taken in something that is short-lived (*De causa aff.* 8.14 Helmreich).

The continuum felt between the *hôra* of nature and of the young is expressed in other ways, too. During the lovemaking between Zeus and Hera in the *Iliad* (14.300–351), the earth responds by sending up fresh grass, dewy lotusflowers, and an abundance of soft crocuses and hyacinths. The elemental powers of nature and human love are both reflections of life flourishing.[5] Odysseus likens Nausicaa to a tender plant (*Od.* 6.163), and Sappho makes the same association with a bridegroom (fr. 115). She compares a young girl to a sweet red apple (fr. 105a) or to a hyacinth (fr. 105b).

Greek metaphor (like English) reflected this continuum: Youth is described as a "flowering" (e.g., *Il.* 13.484), and girls come into the "flowering of their maidenhood" (*H. Dem.* 108). It is, of course, not surprising that *charis* enters into this context: Youth is "full of *charis*" (Anacreon fr. 395.3, cf. *Od.* 10.279 = *Il.* 24.348). *Charis*, which depicted the allurement of the *hôra* or the *hêbê*, disappeared when this moment had passed, like the fading of delicate spring flowers or the hyacinth that is trampled under the treading feet of shepherds (Sappho, fr. 105b).[6] In the Cologne Epode of Archilochus (fr. 196a27–28), Neobule is described as having lost the "bloom of her maidenhood" and thereby "the *charis* that was on it before." This *charis* was connected with the freshness of youth, which dried up with old age or with

[5] For a discussion of sympathetic nature in the love-context, see Treu 1955, 203–5.

[6] Irwin 1984, 152, writes, "Flowers bloom for a short time before they fade. Even in their beauty they appear vulnerable. The fleeting moment of perfection passes, sometimes hastened by natural events or people's carelessness, and they die. So the death of the young, and particularly of young warriors, is commemorated by flowers in cult and poetry."

sexual excess.[7] Occurring at the *hôra*, it was confined to a particular time. Pindar begins his song for Theoxenus with advice to his own *thymos* (his passionate feelings) to respect this measured time of youth's flowering and fruitfulness. Like blossoms and fruits, one "plucks" the fresh object of one's desire at just the right moment:

Χρήν μὲν κατὰ καιρὸν ἐρώτων δρέπεσθαι, θυμέ,
    σὺν ἁλικίᾳ·

One must, my heart, pluck love's fruits in due season, with the ripening of youth.[8]

Pindar fr. 123.1–2

Again, he speaks of the love experience as mutual *charis*-pleasure when it observes the convention of *kairos* (the proper time):

Εἴη καὶ ἐρᾶν καὶ ἔρωτι
χαρίζεσθαι κατὰ καιρόν·
μὴ πρεσβυτέραν ἀριθμοῦ
δίωκε, θυμέ, πρᾶξιν.

May it be possible both to love and
to give *charis* in return for love, in due season;
do not, my heart, pursue a course
that is older than your years.

Pindar fr. 127

One of the special qualities reserved for youth is tenderness. In the Cologne Epode, the girl offers to provide her lusty suitor with a "tender (*tereina*) maiden" (6). *Terên* (tender) is used of the soft growth of nature, as well as of youth or the young. Sappho invokes the Charites in fr. 128 with another word denoting tenderness, delicacy; the goddesses are *abrai*, once again an epithet equally appropriate for youths and maidens or for vegetation. She confesses to lov-

---

[7] For the importance of moisture to the attractiveness of a beloved, see Brown 1984b, 41n.32.

[8] Cf. "plucking the *hêbê*" (Pindar, *Pyth.* 6.48).

ing such tender lushness (*abrosynê*, fr. 58.25–26). Love opens her up to the sensuality of young growth, in nature and in human beings.

The Charites, fertility goddesses, were venerated for moist tender growth issuing from a fecund earth. It was in springtime for the early Greeks as for us that love and young growth flourished; this was the season to invoke Aphrodite and the Charites.[9] Stesichorus in his *Oresteia* composes a hymn to the Charites, when spring arrives "with the delicacy of new growth," (*habrôs*, fr. 212.2).[10] In the famous *ostrakon* fragment (2), Sappho invites Aphrodite to come to a *charis*-filled apple grove and pour nectar *abrôs*:

.. ανοθεν κατιου[σ-
† δευρυμμεκρητεσιπ[.]ρ[   ]. † ναῦον
ἄγνον, ὄππ[αι   ] χάριεν μὲν ἄλσος
μαλί[αν], βῶμοι δ' ἔ⟨ν⟩ι θυμιάμε-
νοι ⟨λι⟩βανώτω⟨ι⟩·

ἐν δ' ὕδωρ ψῦχρο⌊ν⌋ κελάδει δι' ὔσδων   5
μαλίνων, βρόδοισι δὲ παῖς ὀ χῶρος
ἐσκίαστ', αἰθυσσομένων δὲ φύλλων
κῶμα †καταιριον·

ἐν δὲ λείμων ἰππόβοτος τέθαλε
†τωτ ... (.)ριννοιστ† ἄνθεσιν, αἰ ⟨δ'⟩ ἄηται   10
μέλλιχα πν[έο]ισιν [
[   ]
ἔνθα δὴ σὺ† συ.αν† ἔλοισα, Κύπρι
χρυσίαισιν ἐν κυλίκεσσιν ἄβρως
⟨ὀ⟩μ⟨με⟩μείχμενον θαλίαισι νέκταρ   15
οἰνοχόεισα

Come hither to me to this holy temple
where there is a *charis*-filled grove

[9] See Schadewaldt 1928b, 16, for the association between flourishing vegetation and Aphrodite. West 1970, 317n.28, gives several textual examples linking love and springtime.
[10] This translation takes ἀβρῶς with ἐπερχομένου (see Bowra 1961, 115); others have taken it with ἐξευρόντων or with ὑμνεῖν.

of apple trees, and altars smoking
with incense.

Here cold springs babble past through the
apple branches, and the whole place is shaded
by roses; a heavy drowsiness from the
quivering leaves takes hold of me.

Within, a horse-pasturing meadow is in bloom
with spring flowers; the breezes waft gently . . .

Here do you, Cyprian goddess, take . . .
. . . pour nectar in golden cups with a tender stroke
mingled with the festive rite.

Sappho fr. 2

Sappho's grove, containing spring flowers, shimmering
light, moisture, and sensual lushness is a perfect matrix for
charis, and indeed she is the first to apply the adjective *charieis* to a grove.[11] The milieu is similar to that of the Charites
in Orchomenus, in Pindar's description: Sappho's meadow
is fertile, filled with grazing horses (9, cf.*Ol.* 14.2), and the
powers of Thalia pervade the scene (9, 15).[12] In the fusion of
fecundity, beauty, and tenderness, the ultimate rapture will
take place with the epiphany of the divine.

Sappho's easy familiarity with Aphrodite and the Charites is described by Himerius (*Or.* 94, Sappho fr. 194), where
the poet conducts the rituals of a bridal chamber, decorating
the room with garlands and leading Aphrodite to the scene
in the chariot of the Charites. Hyacinths for Aphrodite,
golden wings and golden hair for Eros, and blazing torches
complete the scene. Flowers, love, and light are the back-
drop for festivities where the Charites perform with Aphrodite. These are Sappho's *thaliai*, rites of heightened desire.

[11] Noted by Treu 1955, 212.

[12] West 1970, 317: "The θαλίαι are at hand; cups are being filled with
wine. But these θαλίαι are as water that needs the admixture of Aphrodite's
nectar. The cups into which she pours the divine mixture will be cups of
gold; the spirit of love when it comes transfigures everything with heightened sensation."

Like Aphrodite, the Charites are summoned to Sappho's side:

βροδοπάχεες ἄγναι Χάριτες, δεῦτε Δίος κόραι.

Rose-armed holy Charites, (come) hither, daughters of Zeus.

Sappho fr. 53

The epithet "rose-armed" is also used by Sappho to describe Dawn in fr. 58.19. The ancient interpreters explained its application to the Charites as originating with Sappho's love of roses.[13] D. Campbell suggests[14] that Sappho is praising the Charites as "fair-armed" or "white-armed," for she has in mind white roses.

But, as Dawn could claim the epithet "rose-armed" not only on the ground of color (red or white) but also because she brought the day with its flowery growth, so the word may not refer to the color of the Charites' arms but to their divine power[15] over the beauty of natural growth, symbolized by roses. Their arms are no more rosy than the moon of fr. 96 is rosy-fingered (8), spreading its glow over sea and land. Beauty stimulates desire and fecundity. The moon's beauty sheds dewy moisture over fields that consequently bloom with roses and tender flowery growth. Just like the moon, the Charites, by their beauty stimulate new life. In the *Anacreontea* (55.21) nymphs, like Sappho's Charites, are described as "rose-armed." Nymphs, the Charites and Aphrodite were all associated with nurturing and preparing the young for the

---

[13] E.g., Philostratus (*Ep.* 51): "Sappho loves the rose and always crowns it with some praise, likening to it the beauty of her maidens; she likens it also to the arms of the Charites, when she describes their naked arms."

[14] Campbell 1967, 280n.8.

[15] ἄγνος is a strong epithet, associated with divine majesty: Rudhardt 1958, 40; Gerber 1965, 212–13, points out that ἀγνὰ δῶρα were gifts that inspired awe and could have dire consequences. Gentili 1984, 285–94, discusses the implication of this adjective, which is applied to Sappho herself in a fragment attributed to Alcaeus (fr. 384). Gentili points to the appropriateness of ἄγναι with Charites, because of their chthonic powers as vegetation goddesses (293). Sappho, he argues, earns the title because of her affinity with goddesses like the Charites and Aphrodite.

rites of love,[16] often in a garden. Ibycus describes the young Euryalus as a young shoot, "nursling of the Charites" (fr. 288.1) whom Aphrodite and Peitho nurtured in a garden of roses.

It is not surprising, then, to hear Sappho advising the young Dica to crown herself with flowers in the presence of the Charites:

σὺ δὲ στεφάνοις, ὦ Δίκα, π⌋ ἔρθεσ⌊θ᾽ ἐράτοις φόβαισιν
ὄρπακας ἀνήτω συν⟨α⟩⌋ ἑ⌊ρρ⌋ αισ⌋ ᾽ ἀπάλαισι χέρσιν·
εὐάνθεα † γὰρ πέλεται † καὶ Χάριτες μάκαιρα⟨ι⟩
μᾶλλον † προτερην †, ἀστεφανώτοισι δ᾽ ἀπυστρέφονται.

Dica, bind garlands around your lovely locks,
entwining flowery stems of anise with your soft hands;
for the blessed Charites look(?) rather on what is fair-flowered
and turn away from the ungarlanded.

Sappho fr. 81.4–7

If Dica wants to render herself eligible for the gifts of love, to receive the attention of the Charites who will guarantee her success, she must complement the delicacy of her hands with the tender growth of nature.[17]

---

[16] Burnett 1983, 269n.109, cites ancient sources linking Aphrodite, Peitho, the Charites, and Eros with the nurturing characteristics of nymphs, a nurturing that bestowed fertility.

[17] The delicate softness conveyed by ἄπαλος appealed to Sappho. She uses it of the young Gyrinno (fr. 82a), of a tender young girl picking flowers (fr. 122), of a companion on whose breast one might lie (fr. 126), of a neck encircled with flowery garlands (fr. 94.16), and of the soft young growth stimulated by dew in the moonlight (fr. 96.13). The word is found in erotic contexts with other poets as well. In the *Theognidea* (1341) it is the ἁπαλός skin that the poet cannot resist, falling in love against his will. The ἁπαλά hand is found in Alcman (fr. 3.80), where each of the maiden choristers hopes that the beautiful chorus-leader will take her soft hand. Treu 1955, 178–83, points to the vulnerability suggested by Alcman's choice of ἁπαλός here, by contrast to the strength of the hand of Astymelousa. Weakness, vulnerability, etc. is not the element that is dominant in the Sapphic context, however. The word suggests tenderness and refinement (Lasserre 1974, 10–11). This is not to say that the vulnerability disappears; it adds poignancy to the portrait of the virginal Dica.

Just as the Charites and the *charis* of love lure vanished with the passing of the *hêbê* and the *hôra*, so one would not expect to find them in young children. Sappho reveals an exceptional circumstance in the confession that she loved Atthis when Atthis was but a small child and still without *charis*:

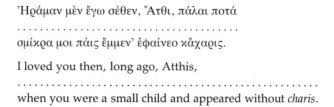

Ἠράμαν μὲν ἔγω σέθεν, Ἄτθι, πάλαι ποτά

....

σμίκρα μοι πάις ἔμμεν' ἐφαίνεο κἄχαρις.

I loved you then, long ago, Atthis,

....

when you were a small child and appeared without *charis*.

Sappho fr. 49

If the two verses were consecutive, Sappho loved Atthis before the young girl reached her *hôra*.[18] What is significant about the passage is that, as a diptych, it provides a *terminus post quem* (in normal circumstances) for erotic *charis*, just as Archilochus' dried-up Neobule provides a *terminus ante quem*.

[18] As cited by the grammarian Terentianus Maurus (6.390 Keil), the verses would appear to be consecutive:

cordi quando fuisse sibi canit Atthida
parvam, florea virginitatis sua cum foret.

(Sappho) sings of Atthis, when she had been dear to her heart, when her maiden flowering was yet to be.

Plutarch gives only the second verse, glossing it with the explanation that ἄχαρις indicated "the young girl had not yet reached the *hôra* of marriage" (τὴν οὔπω γάμων ἔχουσαν ὥραν, *Amat.* 751d). Plato gives us perhaps an unconscious recollection of Sappho's reflection at *Charm.* 154B. The handsome young Charmides is about to arrive, and Socrates recalls that he found him attractive even when he was a young boy: οὐ γάρ τι φαῦλος οὐδὲ τότε ἦν ἔτι παῖς ὤν, νῦν δ' οἶμαί που εὖ μάλα ἂν ἤδη μειράκιον εἴη. (He was in no wise common-looking then, when he was still a boy. Now, I imagine, he would be an exceedingly beautiful stripling.) Socrates goes on to confess that he is no judge of beauty; he finds all youths at this age beautiful.

The love lure of *charis* dwelt particularly in the eyes. In Hesiod's *Theogony* the Charites "drip love from their eyes" (910). Alcman calls them "love-eyed" (fr. 1.20–21). Beautiful women had the "eye-sparkle" of the Charites. Sappho asks a friend, who is quite conscious of his beauty (according to Athenaeus 13.564d), to shed over her the *charis* that is on his eyes:

στᾶθι † κἄντα † φίλος
καὶ τὰν ἐπ᾿ ὄσσοισ᾿ ὀμπέτασον χάριν.

Stand facing me, friend,
and spread out the *charis* that is on your eyes.

Sappho fr. 138

Sappho uses the imperative *ompetasai* (*anapetannymi*) in addressing the fellow. If the verb is understood as "unfolding," "unfurling," (parallels can be found in *Il.* 1.480 and Eur. *Hipp.* 202), Sappho is thinking of *charis* here as something corporeal, a sort of love canopy that could be draped over the two of them. But the verb can also be used with light, in the sense of "emanate" or "radiate" (e.g., Eur. *IA* 34), and in another context (fr. 16) Sappho associates light with the beauty that arouses desire.[19] In fr. 16, her priamel on behalf of love, it is the bright sparkle of Anactoria's face which she longs to see, rejecting in favor of this all other standard exemplars of beauty. In fr. 138, Sappho could be extending a challenge to the handsome fellow to charm her with the love light of his eyes.

According to early Greek theories of perception, the eye was the source of a ray of light—of fire—that was necessary for vision.[20] As eyes beamed, so they saw, hence the single

[19] For a discussion of this association, see Koniaris 1967, 257–68.

[20] Alcmaeon of Croton (late sixth c. B.C.E.) devised the earliest theory of perception of which a record has survived. Theophrastus records him as saying that the eyes see through a fluid that surrounds them, a liquid that possesses fire (Alkmaion 14 A 5DK = Theophrastus *de Sensu* 25). The same notion of perception is reflected in the poets. In Hesiod's *Theogony* Typhoeus flashes forth a "wondrous fire" from his eyes (826–27). Pindar describes himself as "looking brightness with his eye" (*Nem.* 7.66).

act of beaming and seeing could not fail to affect the person who was the object of the illuminated/illuminating gaze. *Charis*, when it was found on the eyes with *aidôs*, as in the epiphany of Demeter to Metaneira, commanded respect and deference. When it was the *charis* of love being transmitted by the light gaze of the eyes, a response in kind was difficult to avoid. Pindar's Theoxenus has eyes that flare as he looks, and Pindar cannot help but react:

τὰς δὲ Θεοξένου ἀκτῖνας πρὸς ὄσσων
μαρμαρυζοίσας δρακείς
ὃς μὴ πόθῳ κυμαίνεται

Who does not swell with desire, catching sight of
the rays of light that flash from the eyes of Theoxenus?

Pindar fr. 123.2–3

Marmaryzô is a light-verb that connotes more than a sparkle: It is used of the gleam of bronze weaponry in Homer and the lightning bolt in Hesiod (*Theog.* 699). Sophocles, in a fragment preserved in Athenaeus 564b (= fr. 474 Radt) describes Pelops as having a similar look, a dazzling "lightning glance"; when he looks at Hippodameia, he is "inflamed" but she is "scorched." Sophocles describes the visual firelink between lover and beloved as a plumb line.[21]

At the departure of one of the love partners, the *charis* that is connected with this love-flash from the eyes disappears. When Helen left for Troy, Menelaus' eyes, as they looked at

---

According to Aristotle, Empedocles took the theory one stage further, with the notion of emanations coming from objects seen, at the same time as the eye's fire sends a ray forth that beams upon the object (Empedocles 21B 84DK= Arist. *de Sensu* 2.437b23). On this analysis the experience of seeing and being seen is one light-event; the subjective and the objective are fused.

[21] Pearson 1917, 129, elaborates as follows: "The fiery flash is a physical emanation from the eye, which, making its way straight to the eye of the beloved, is met in its course by the responsive glance of mutual love speeding as fast to the eye of the lover." For a general association of love with the eyes, see West 1966, *ad* 910.

cold statues in her stead, lacking a responsive return-gaze, stared emptily:

εὐμόρφων δὲ κολοσσῶν
ἔχθεται χάρις ἀνδρί,
ὀμμάτων δ' ἐν ἀχηνίαις
    ἔρρει πᾶσ''Αφροδίτα.

The *charis* of shapely statues
is hateful to the husband,
and in the empty gaze of the eyes
all of Aphrodite's charm vanished.

Aeschylus *Ag.* 416–19

A small corpus of erotic poetry is found in the second book of the Theognidean collection of elegies. These one hundred fifty-eight verses, although composed by various archaic poets,[22] are more or less consistent in tone, very different from Sappho. They do not celebrate love; instead, they address its conventions. Whereas the departure of a beloved is an occasion for a sensual recollection of love's poignancy in Aeschylus or in Sappho, in the Theognidean collection this is denounced as a betrayal.

The *charis* of beauty figures but once in the ephebic love-relationships that are the subject of this poetry. It occurs in an elegy in which the poet-lover can double his appeal to a young beloved by punning on two applications of the word *charis*:

῏Ω παῖ, ἐπεί τοι δῶκε θεὰ χάριν ἱμερόεσσαν
    Κύπρις, σὸν δ' εἶδος πᾶσι νέοισι μέλει,
τῶνδ' ἐπάκουσον ἐπῶν καὶ ἐμὴν χάριν ἔνθεο θυμῷ
    γνοὺς ἔρος ὡς χαλεπὸν γίνεται ἀνδρὶ φέρειν.

Boy, since the goddess Cypris has given you the *charis* that arouses desire, and your beauty is the focus of all young men,

---

[22] These include Theognis himself and Solon. See West 1974, 43, where he concludes that none of the poems appears to be later than the fifth century B.C.E.

FIGURE 3. *Symposiast*, on a Red-figure *kylix*, fifth century B.C.E. A man is shown reclining on a couch stroking a hare (a love gift between homosexual lovers) and singing *o paidon kalliste* ("Oh, handsomest of boys").

> hear my words and put my *charis* in your heart,
> knowing how difficult a thing love is for a man to bear.
>
> *Theognis* 1319–1322

The poet's intent is to persuade the boy to comply with his wishes. To do this, he begins with a flattering reference to the boy's beauty (*charis*, cf. "Oh, handsomest of boys," Fig. 3), then links this with his own gratification (*charis*). The repetition of the word in the same position in both hexameters underscores the fact that the pleasure requested (*charin* 1321) is in fact the possession of the boy's desirable body (*charin* 1319).

It is the *charis* that should gratify both partners in a relationship that motivates much of this poetry. The beloved receives gifts from the lover; in return, the lover expects the pleasure of sexual satisfaction and the further gratification of respectful attention paid to him by the younger boy. The word used for this is *aidôs*, combined, as in other contexts, with *charis*:

Ὦ παῖ, ὃς εὖ ἔρδοντι κακὴν ἀπέδωκας ἀμοιβήν,
   οὐδέ τις ἀντ' ἀγαθῶν ἐστι χάρις παρὰ σοί·
οὐδέν πώ μ' ὤνησας· ἐγὼ δέ σε πολλάκις ἤδη
   εὖ ἔρδων αἰδοῦς οὐδεμιῆς ἔτυχον.

Boy, you who requite evil in exchange to one who has favored
   you,
nor has there been any *charis* from you in return for good
   things given:
in no wise to date have you been of benefit to me. Often I,
although treating you kindly, encountered no trace of *aidôs*.

Theognis 1263–66

The lover berates the boy because he has not observed the conventions of reciprocity in their relationship. The elder partner invested not only money, in the form of gifts to the boy, but attention, providing the boy with protection and instruction.[23] In return he can expect *aidôs*, a certain deference from the boy to his lover's wishes. No doubt this entailed sexual favors, as is made clear in another elegy that combines *aidôs* and *charis*:

αἴδεό μ', ὦ παῖ, διδοὺς χάριν, εἴ ποτε καὶ σὺ
   ἕξεις Κυπρογενοῦς δῶρον ἰοστεφάνου
χρηΐζων καὶ ἐπ' ἄλλον ἐλεύσεαι·

Show me *aidôs*, boy, giving me *charis*,
If ever you, too, will have the gift of violet-crowned
   Aphrodite,
And, full of desire, will be chasing after someone else in turn.

Theognis 1331–33

[23] Dover 1978, 92, 202.

The syntax makes it clear that the awarding of *aidôs* consists in the giving of *charis*, and that this is, specifically, the satisfaction brought by the "gift of Aphrodite." In other literary contexts, particularly in comedy, sexual favor is the bald reference of *charis* or *charites*.[24] But *aidôs* implies more. It suggests that the compliance is of broader compass, embracing not only the body but the feelings of the lover, providing the attenuated pleasures of deference and constancy.[25] When a partner did not observe this code, he was violating the convention that required good for good. This was an "evil exchange" (1263, above). The system, when it operated successfully, no doubt provided a successful model for the reciprocity that characterized living in a healthy social community: It was an important part of the *paideia* received by the young boy.[26] When the youth did not comply, the angry adult, like Achilles, withdrew his services:

ἐκλέλυμαι δὲ πόθου πρὸς ἐϋστεφάνου Κυθερείης
σοὶ δ' ὦ παῖ χάρις ἔστ' οὐδεμία πρὸς ἐμοῦ.

I am released from the desire that comes from fair-garlanded
   Cytherea;
And for you, boy, there will be no *charis* from me.

Theognis 1339–40

---

[24] Vetta 1980, 68, *ad* 1264 gives several examples from comedy where χάρις refers directly to sexual gratification.

[25] The constancy expected of the love from a boy-beloved, described as *charis* in the elegy of vv. 1367–1368, is contrasted with the fickle nature of woman love. The boy who displays such lack of constancy is denounced in 1373–74. This type of misogyny, based upon a mistrust of the fidelity of women, was a topos in Greek literature, beginning with Homer and Hesiod (see Vetta 1980, 139 for examples). Perhaps the most famous example is Semonides' diatribe against women (fr.7).

[26] For the usefulness of erotic *paideia* as a means of social control, see Lewis 1985, 197–222. Vetta 1980, 67, points out the rapport between χάρις operating in the erotic sphere, where it designates reciprocity and fidelity, and the obligations implicit in the χάρις of the *polis*, the political code of the elite.

The code of homosexual love obeyed the constraints of *dikê*: Non-compliance met with reprisals. These could be immediate, in the form of the loss of a lover's *charis*, or they could be more long-term. The youth will one day be pursuing his own beloved, and Aphrodite is presumed to deal with his desire at that time as he had once treated his own lover (1332–33 above). This same attenuated justice in love is presumed by Sappho in fr. 1, and again it is Aphrodite who will exact reprisals. The love goddess assures the poet that the noncompliant beloved who flees her advances, rejects her gifts, violating *dikê* (20), will one day fall in love even against her will, as she in her turn pursues and offers gifts to another.[27] Bringing the case of Theognis or of Sappho into the divine sphere is more than poetic fantasy. It is a consequence of the pervasiveness of the code of requital, in which *charis* participated, whether on the couch or the battlefield. On the couch, Aphrodite enforced it.

The homosexual love-partnership was not symmetrical and yet it depended upon reciprocity, like the relationship between the Homeric commander and his soldiers or that between men and gods. The lovers tried to redress this asymmetry, however, by posturing as suppliants[28] or as slaves.[29] In the love chase the quarry could refuse to be caught. When this happened, the Theognidean poet-lover used language that once again reflected the congruity of the

---

[27] For a discussion of this, see Giacomelli 1980, 135–42. The Theognidean poet of 1283–94 prefaces his lament about the love chase with ὦ παῖ, μή μ' ἀδίκει ("Oh boy, don't commit an injustice against me.")

[28] For a defence of the restoration of ἱκέτις, "suppliant," to the homoerotic lines of Alcman fr. 3.81, a defence that is based on this posturing, see Davies 1986, 13–14.

[29] Plato, *Symp.* 183a (Pausanias): οἱ ἐρασταί . . . ἱκετείας . . . ποιούμενοι . . . καὶ ἐθέλοντες δουλείας δουλεύειν οἵας οὐδ' ἂν δοῦλος οὐδείς (lovers making supplication . . . and willingly enduring such slavery as not even a slave would tolerate). Halperin 1986, 129–35, makes the important point that Plato had Socrates in the *Symposium* break through this posturing of inequality, to demonstrate that balanced erotic reciprocity could mirror the reciprocal dynamic of dialectic and motivate erotic desire for philosophical inquiry.

erotic and the broader social code: The boy is "greedy" (1301), his behavior is "savage," "uncivilized" (1302), wanting in *charis* (1303).

And yet the intensity of the experience, whether the quarry is caught or not, brought its own pleasurable reward, described as a *charis* by the poet of 1369–72, in one of the very few moments in the collection where one senses an honest personal disclosure:

μυρία δ' ἐξ αὐτοῦ κρέμαται κακά, μυρία δ' ἐσθλά·
ἀλλ' ἔν τοι † ταύτῃ καί τις ἔνεστι χάρις.

A thousand evils hang from the game of love, a thousand goods;
But within, after all, there is some *charis* attached to it as well.

Theognis 1371–72

Chapter Five

SOCIAL *CHARIS*

οὔτις αἰδοῖος μετ᾽ ἀστῶν οὐδὲ περίφημος θανὼν
γίνεται· χάριν δὲ μᾶλλον τοῦ ζοοῦ διώκομεν
<οἱ>ζοοί, κάκιστα δ᾽ αἰεὶ τῷ θανόντι γίνεται.

No one, once he is dead, receives *aidôs* from his
townsmen, nor is he talked about in public.
Rather we, the living, pursue the *charis* of the living,
and it always turns out worst for the one who is dead.
Archilochus fr. 133

THIS POEM is preoccupied with the *charis*-pleasure of
a chase that is different from the love chase. Archilochus describes the pursuit of popular acclaim as a
circuit chase, where only living participants qualify: Townsmen contend for and award each other *aidôs*, which is accompanied by the pleasure of hearing their name in general
circulation.[1] This is a secular combination of *charis* and *aidôs*;
they are not associated with mortals' entering the divine
presence (Demeter) or experiencing the paralyzing power
of love (Pandora). In the case of Demeter or Pandora, we are
witnessing human encounters that are vertical, social en-
gagements with a power greater than oneself, and indeed
much of the pleasure comes from just that sense of the
verticality of the connection. But the link that concerns Archilochus is a horizontal one, connecting peers—townspeople who encountered each other on the street. They vied
with each other to be talked about not as notorious but as

---

[1] The circularity of this chase for *charis* is reflected in the ambiguity of
Archilochus' syntax. τοῦ ζοοῦ after χάριν can be a subjective or an objective
genitive: χάριν δὲ . . . τοῦ ζοοῦ διώκομεν can mean "we pursue the *charis*
from the living" or "for the living."

worthy of respect, *aidôs*. This was a social milieu much pre-occupied with a sense of one's worth or *timê;* recitations of the *Iliad* would keep alive the example of Achilles.

In the world of Archilochus, although people were less concerned with heroic behavior, they still looked to their peers for a spoken assessment of their worth. At death one's name, hence oneself, was silenced and the anonymity of this condition was a very dreary prospect. An expression of the same sentiment is found in Stesichorus:

θανόντος ἀνδρὸς πᾶσα † πολιὰ † ποτ' ἀνθρώπων χάρις.

All *charis* from people, for a man who has died, grows hoary-white.

Stesichorus fr. 245

This fragment, preserved in Stobaeus with the uncertain *polia* ("hoary, grey-white") is glossed by Arsenius (II 455L-S) as "all *charis* from people perishes for a man when he dies."

This is the *charis*-pleasure that can be characterized as social, confined to the members of a community that created and contained the name, position, and reputation of its living members. In this milieu, pleasure was in large measure derived from the giving and taking of favors. Sophocles in the *Ajax* captures the moment when this all-important reciprocal obligation is dissolved. The hero Ajax, who had performed a multitude of military favors for his king Agamemnon, has died, and his brother Teucer speaks angrily about the king who no longer feels bound to return *charis* in the form of proper burial:

φεῦ, τοῦ θανόντος ὡς ταχεῖά τις βροτοῖς
χάρις διαρρεῖ καὶ προδοῦσ' ἁλίσκεται

Alas! With what speed the *charis* of mortals flows away from a
man who has died
And, as a traitor, is caught in the act

Sophocles *Ajax* 1266–67

Agamemnon, prior recipient of Ajax's *charis*, is the betrayer. He ignores his return obligation because he will no longer encounter Ajax. The dead have no active claim on the living. They cannot requite favors, hence are of no social benefit: *Charis* fades from their eyes, that spark of living fire that is set alight by a social encounter:

σπάνιον ἄρ᾽ ἦν θανοῦσιν ἀσφαλεῖς φίλοι
. . . ἡ δ᾽ ἐν ὀφθαλμοῖς χάρις
ἀπόλωλ᾽, ὅταν τις ἐκ δόμων ἀνὴρ θάνῃ.

A scarce thing indeed was evidence of friends who remained steadfast to the departed . . .
The *charis* on the eyes perished, whenever some man died (and was taken) from the house.

Euripides fr. 736.3–6 N

The eye spark, which in other contexts inflamed desire, is here connected with the beauty inspired by the fidelity of friendship. Sappho addresses the physical beauty of *charis* of the eyes in fr. 138, but she acknowledges in another fragment that moral goodness is also a kind of beauty, of a more abiding sort:

ὁ μὲν γὰρ κάλος ὄσσον ἴδην πέλεται <κάλος>
ὁ δὲ κἄγαθος αὔτικα καὶ κάλος ἔσ<σε>ται.

For one man is handsome inasmuch as he is handsome to see, but another man, a good person, is forthwith handsome and will remain so.

Sappho fr. 50

Semonides, in his diatribe against women (7), distinguishes one, and only one, good wife, the kind of woman who is devoted to her husband and children and who refrains from the licentious chatter in which other women are engaged. She stands out among all the others, because around her "flickers wondrous *charis*" (89). This is the glow of moral, not physical, beauty.

The Charites, exemplars of feminine beauty and charm, also represented the emanation of moral beauty. The first book of the Theognidean corpus, which consists largely of advice about appropriate behavior, is prefaced by a poem addressed to the Muses and Charites. These goddesses, the poet says, sang a "beautifully worded phrase" (16) at the wedding of Cadmus and Harmonia. The beautiful phrase was itself concerned with beauty:

ὅττι καλὸν φίλον ἐστί, τὸ δ᾽ οὐ καλὸν οὐ φίλον ἐστί

Whatever is beautiful is beloved, and what is not beautiful is not beloved.

Theognis 17

Although this reference to beauty doubtless signals aesthetic praise of the collection of verses that follows,[2] the next poem in the collection stresses the poet's pride in the ethical value of his poetry. The quality of his work, Theognis claims, is unimpeachable on both aesthetic and moral grounds. As the presence of the Charites assured the attractiveness (17) of his words, so they presided over the beautiful behavior he recommended. And Cyrnus, the young beloved to whom Theognis directed his advice, would be under their protection, attractive because beautiful in both a moral and physical sense.

But Cyrnus, it turns out, falls far short of this ideal, and most of the elegies in the collection address the lack of *charis*, of beautiful behavior, in the boy or in people referred to as *deiloi* ("worthless") or *kakoi* ("vile"). In the poem beginning at 1135, the Charites abandon human company, departing for Olympus with *Pistis* (Faithfulness) and *Sophrosynê* (Moderation). These are both social qualities. Although *sophro-*

---

[2] Van Groningen 1966 *ad loc.* points to the "valeur esthétique" of this poem and conjectures that it does not refer to the poetry that follows, but was taken from a symposium where there was a discussion of art. This remains a conjecture, and the quatrain containing the Charites' song could have been composed simply to introduce and highlight this collection of elegies, much like the proems of the *Homeric Hymns.* Plato (*Lys.* 216C) refers to the expression τὸ καλὸν φίλον as proverbial. Levine 1985, 176–77, recalls the significance of the Charites at a wedding, where there would be communal eating and drinking. He sees this as a metaphor for the ἁρμονίη of political integration, the social cohesion of a well-ordered *polis* which is the focus of much of the poetry of Book I. On the background of this, see Hudson-Williams 1910, 6–12, and West, 1974, 65–71.

synê in early Greek literature referred to an individual's sound-mindedness, it quickly became a social, not a private, virtue, similar in meaning to *aidôs*, the opposite of *hybris* ("arrogant insensitivity to others").[3] Refusing to recognize the needs and rights of others, refusing to moderate one's selfish desires and to exercise *sophrosynê*, one could expect to lose the patrons of *charis*. Further, contracts between people were no longer kept (1139), explaining the departure of Faithfulness. With the loss of this social virtue the Charites, patrons of reciprocal dealings between individuals, must leave. The passage appears to be a direct recollection of Hesiod's Iron Age. In this age one cannot expect to see the *charis* of the man who is faithful to his oath, observant of justice, says Hesiod (*Op*.190). Similarly, the poet in the Theognidean collection makes it clear that the departure of the Charites signals the loss of faithful, just oaths.[4] This is a serious social breakdown.[5] Oaths bind people together; without *charis* or the Charites, there can be no such bonds.

For ties between people to be lasting, the individuals concerned must remember the advantages of these ties and respond in kind to gestures of goodwill from others. This was made explicit in the bargaining between Hera and Hypnos at *Iliad* 14.233–76. Remembering a favor implies acknowledging and reciprocating it. This social sequence, practiced by gods, heroes, and Theognis' good class of people, is the mark of encounters that are mutually satisfying, and it breeds a train of good deeds. These encounters gener-

---

[3] See North 1966, 16–19. In his Partheneion (fr. 1), Alcman denounces the hybristic aspirations of men against the gods. Like the Theognidean description, the Charites are described as entering the house of Zeus (20–21). The passage is lacunose, but the *hybris* of mortals and the removal of the Charites to Olympus are in all likelihood connected.

[4] ὅρκοι δ' οὐκέτι πιστοὶ ἐν ἀνθρώποισι δίκαιοι (there are no longer faithful, just oaths among people, 1139), cf. οὐδέ τις εὐόρκου χάρις ἔσσεται οὐδὲ δικαίου (there will be no *charis* of a well-kept oath nor of a just one, *Op*. 190).

[5] For a discussion of the sociopolitical implications of the departure of the Charites at Theognis 1138, see Levine 1985, 176–77.

ate others; they are fertile. On the other hand, the behavior of the vile and worthless people (the *kakoi* or the *deiloi*) is sterile; these individuals have a memory only for offenses committed, not for kindnesses:

δειλοὺς δ' εὖ ἔρδοντι ματαιοτάτη χάρις ἐστίν·   105
ἶσον καὶ σπείρειν πόντον ἁλὸς πολιῆς·
οὔτε γὰρ ἂν πόντον σπείρων βαθὺ λήιον ἀμῷς,
οὔτε κακοὺς εὖ δρῶν εὖ πάλιν ἀντιλάβοις.

ἄπληστον γὰρ ἔχουσι κακοὶ νόον· ἢν δ' ἓν ἁμάρτῃς
τῶν πρόσθεν πάντων ἐκκέχυται φιλότης.   110
οἱ δ' ἀγαθοὶ τὸ μέγιστον ἐπαυρίσκουσι παθόντες
μνῆμα δ' ἔχουσ' ἀγαθῶν καὶ χάριν ἐξοπίσω.

The *charis* returned to a benefactor of the worthless ones is of
  the most trifling sort;   105
this is equal to sowing seeds in a sea of grey brine.
For you would not harvest a heavy crop by sowing on the sea,
nor in doing favors to the vile sort would you get back good
  in return.

The vile ones have an insatiable disposition. If once you slip,
the good feeling from all those previous kindnesses ebbs
  away.   110
But the good sort are aware to the highest degree[6] of what
  they have experienced,
retaining the memory only of the good deeds done, and
  showing *charis* thereafter.

Theognis 105–12

Like Hera and Hypnos, who will remember their favors exchanged "for all time," Theognis' good class of people allow this memory to define their social relationships. Peccadilloes are ignored in order to sustain a bond that is abiding and fertile. *Charis* registers in the memory *thereafter*.

 Charis occurs several times in Book I of the *Theognidea*,

---

[6] For the various suggestions that have been put forth to translate μέγιστον ἐπαυρίσκουσι, see van Groningen 1966 *ad loc.*

always as a characteristic of the good sort of people, the *agathoi*, and as a quality lacking in the vile, the *deiloi*. The same language is found in the erotic elegies of Book II. A lover who gets no returns from the *charis* he showed his boy beloved is just like the benefactor who was abused by an ungrateful recipient:

εἴ τι παθὼν ἀπ' ἐμεῦ ἀγαθὸν μέγα μὴ χάριν οἶδας,
    χρῄζων ἡμετέρους αὖθις ἵκοιο δόμους.

If you have enjoyed some great good thing from me and not
    acknowledged the *charis*,
Would that you would come to my house again in crying
    need.

Theognis 957–58

The deepest gratification for human beings comes from the satisfaction of a need or desire. If satisfaction is refused, the same emotional intensity is directed at retaliation, if possible in kind. A recipient of a favor who leaves his benefactor empty-handed will be made needy in return, (*chrêizôn*, 958). Similarly, in the erotic elegies of Book II, the boy-beloved is reminded that a type of justice operates to retaliate with shame for shame, loss for loss. Like his lover, the boy will be full of desire one day but will be left wanting in his desire for reciprocal gratification (*chrêizôn*, 1333). Responding to a lover is like responding to a benefactor: You owe priority of attention. In both contexts this is expressed as "giving place to the *charis*" of the donor (1096, 1321).

The identification of inconsiderate behavior (behavior that did not demonstrate *charis*) with an undesirable group in the populace, the *deiloi*, became proverbial. Advice to shun these *deiloi*, on the grounds that they offer no *charis*-returns, was framed in a proverbial song generally attributed to the Thessalian king Admetus:

Ἀδμήτου λόγον ὦ ἑταῖρε μαθὼν τοὺς ἀγαθοὺς φίλει,
    τῶν δειλῶν δ' ἀπέχου γνοὺς ὅτι δειλῶν ὀλίγα χάρις.

My friend, heed the advice of Admetus and consort with the
   good ones;
keep your distance from the worthless ones, knowing
   that from the worthless comes scant *charis*.

Praxilla 749 (cf. Carm. Conv. 897)

The *agathoi*, who practiced this form of enlightened self-
interest that maintained a stable community, were adhering
to the same code practiced on the Homeric battlefield. This
do ut des practice was the foundation of *koinônia* (common
fellowship), the core of Greek society. Giving one another
what each was due saved the society from anarchy. Behavior
that did not conform to this pattern was intemperate,
greedy, selfish. Plato calls this *pleonexia*, "claiming more
than one's share" (*Gorgias* 508a). The cosmos, the gods, and
mortals are bound rather, he says, by the principles of common fellowship and friendship, by order, moderation, and
justice—those social qualities that were lacking in Theognis'
Megara. Plato describes the cosmos as composed of a kind
of geometric equality, of which greed is a serious violation.

The advantages of this were, of course, readily demon-
strable. Hesiod warns, "Measure fairly what you take from
a neighbor, and pay him back fairly in the same measure, or
better if you can, so that if you are in need you will find him
a sure help in the future" (*Op.* 349–51). The visibility of life in
archaic Greece meant that the nature of reciprocal transactions would be public knowledge and a source of public
honor or shame.[7]

Charis, a pleasure that was invariably social, was deeply
wedded to the experience of *koinônia* when one felt the joy of
community, intensified by its reflection in others. The *polis*
depended on reciprocity, as Aristotle pointed out: Because
exchange bound people together, a shrine of the Charites

---

[7] This had important implications for Solon's reforms and for the agrarian crisis in Attica in the seventh and sixth centuries B.C.E. (Gallant 1982,
111–24).

should be set up in a public place, to remind people to reciprocate kindness (*NE* 5.1133a).[8]

Archilochus plays upon the obligatory returns that his audience would associate with the word *charis* as well as with *xeinia* (guest-gifts), to produce some stunning verbal abuse:

ξείνια δυσμενέσιν λυγρὰ χαριζόμενοι

Giving the *charis* of baneful guest-gifts to the enemy.

Archilochus fr. 6

The ironic play on these words[9] foreshadows such phrases as *acharis charis*, the *charis* that is no *charis*, found later in Greek tragedy.

The symposium was one setting where the gratification produced by mutual give-and-take among friends would be felt most keenly. For this communal pleasure, it was essential to avoid the excesses of behavior that resulted from drunkenness. The poet of verses 467–96 in the Theognidean collection (who may be Evenus) points out the vices of abusing wine, the drink most full of *charis*-pleasure when consumed in moderation (477–78). Excessive drinking robs one of *aidôs* (482), making the tongue abusive of others, saying shameful things that destroy the fellowship (479–83). Keeping strife away from the symposium was vital (494), and he who kept his tongue under control was the symposiast victor (491–92). An aggressive tongue would fracture the communal pleasure, depriving the symposium of *charis* (496).

---

[8] Aristotle is careful, however, to make clear the distinction between reciprocity and equality: The distribution of power and resources in the *polis* of his time is explicitly hierarchical, and the give-and-take of favors is calculated with this in mind, a refinement of the calculation based on one's due portion.

[9] It may well be a direct transmission of the Homeric irony in *Od.* 9.356, where Polyphemus asks Odysseus to tell him his name so he may give him the ξείνιον he had requested, something in which he may take χάρις-pleasure (ἵνα τοι δῶ ξείνιον ᾧ κε σὺ χαίρῃς). This guest-gift is the privilege of being eaten last. See Lavelle 1981, 197–99.

Such behavior had been described by Hesiod as "rough and stormy" (*Op.* 722), and calmness, like the untroubled sea, characterized the ideal symposium. Balance and justice are its hallmarks: Xenophanes gives us the best-known formula for a successful symposium, and with this he advises that during the preliminary libations one pray for the power to perform only "just and fair actions" (B 1.15–16).

Dikê, the equilibrium produced by different, even opposing, forces, which results in the calmness of the symposium, also characterizes a city at peace. When Xenophanes gives the appropriate subjects for sympotic discourse, he cautions against accounts of violent civil discord, for this is of no use or benefit. Similarly, when the poet of the Theognidean elegy 757–64 prays for a city under the shadow of a threatened invasion by the Persians, he asks for Apollo to set the citizens' tongues straight, so that they may all drink while "enjoying *charis*-filled conversation with one another" (763).[10] In the social setting of the symposium, it is the moderation of the tongue (guaranteed by moderation in drink) that ensures the presence of *charis*. This minicommunity, which observed *dikê*, maintaining mutual *aidôs*, was a social gathering where Thalia would dominate. A fragment attributed to Hesiod describes the "flourishing" pleasure of the feast when, after eating, the guests take enjoyment in speech:

ἡδύ ἐστιν . . .
   ἐν δαιτὶ καὶ εἰλαπίνῃ τεθαλυίῃ
τέρπεσθαι μύθοισιν, ἐπὴν δαιτὸς κορέσωνται

It is sweet . . . at table and at the flourishing feast
to take pleasure in words, when they are satisfied with the banquet.

Hesiod fr. 274

[10] For a fuller discussion of the importance of peace to the symposium and to the *polis*, and of the link between the two social units, see Bielohlawek 1940, 11–30; Slater 1981, 205–14; and Seng 1988, 123–31, with bibliography in n.18, 126.

Describing the feast as "flourishing" reflected the priority given to the enjoyment of human exchange and common experience, when these were harmonious. Social harmony was guaranteed by restraint not only in conversation but also in the words of the songs or poems that would be heard.

Dionysius Chalcus describes a symposium where he passes a poem to another guest as "mixing the *charites* of the Charites." The recipient of the poem is expected to respond with a song:

δέχου τήνδε προπινομένην
τὴν ἀπ' ἐμοῦ ποίησιν· ἐγὼ δ' ἐπιδέξια πέμπω
σοὶ πρώτῳ, Χαρίτων ἐγκεράσας χάριτας.
καὶ σὺ λαβὼν τόδε δῶρον ἀοιδὰς ἀντιπρόπιθι,
συμπόσιον κοσμῶν καὶ τὸ σὸν εὖ θέμενος.

Take this poem, pledged and presented to you
by me. I'm sending it to you first, passing it right,
mixing the *charites* of the Charites.
You take this gift and pledge me songs in return,
adorning the symposium and having a care for your own
well-being.

Dionysius Chalcus fr. 1

The image behind these words is a complex one. The *charites* of the Charites are described as if they were the wine, which would be mixed in appropriate measure for harmonious drinking at the symposium.[11] With the ingredients properly blended, the host raises a poetic toast (1), holding up his poem like a cup of wine, and he is entitled to a reciprocal gift in the form of a return toast-poem (4). The experience is reciprocal, the pleasure mutual, and the poems are correctly

[11] Hesiod describes the correct measure as three parts water to one part wine (*Op.* 596). See West 1978 *ad loc.* for a discussion of this and other mixtures. For the "blending" that is characteristic of a symposium of the Charites, cf. the scolion (917b *PMG*) where the *crater* of the Charites is garlanded, and wine and words are mixed.

blended. In this way public and private pleasure are one and the same (5), and the poems can correctly be called *charites* of the Charites.

The sixteenth *Idyll* of Theocritus is simply called "Charites." The goddesses represent the poet's compositions. They are woven into an elaborate but transparent appeal to the tyrant Hieron to remunerate Theocritus for his poems. "Who," he asks, "of as many as dwell under the bright dawn, will open his doors and gladly welcome home our *Charites* and not send them away again unrewarded?" (5–7). The *Charites*-poems become the Charites-goddesses, who return from their quest barefoot and starved and reproach the poet for a fruitless journey (8–12). This *prosopopoeia* represents a *triple entendre*[12] on the word *charites*. It stands for Theocritus' poetry and the goddesses who preside over it.[13] But in addition, by performing the function of seeking payment for the poems they embody, the *Charites* represent reciprocal *charis*, the pleasure generated by praise poetry, where the honoring of a patron is rewarded with money.

The whole is a clever reworking of the poet's dilemma purportedly described by Simonides, preserved in the scholiast on Theocritus' poem but also in the following form by Stobaeus:

Σιμωνίδην παρακαλοῦντός τινος ἐλκώμιον ποιῆσαι καὶ χάριν ἕξειν λέγοντος, ἀργύριον δὲ μὴ διδόντος "δύο" εἶπεν οὗτος "ἔχω κιβωτούς, τὴν μὲν χαρίτων τὴν δὲ ἀργυρίου· καὶ πρὸς τὰς χρείας τὴν μὲν τῶν χαρίτων κενὴν εὑρίσκω, ὅταν ἀνοίξω, τὴν δὲ χρήσιμον μονήν."

Someone asked Simonides to compose a praise song for him, and said that he would receive *charis*. But when he didn't give him any silver, Simonides said, "I have two containers, one for *charites*, the other for silver. And in time of need, I find the container of *charites* empty when I open it, and the other is the only one of any use."

Stobaeus 10.38

[12] The triple reference is admired by Austin 1967, 11n.19
[13] The double designation for χάρις is adopted by Rist 1978, 146.

The would-be client promises the *charis* of gratitude but does not follow it up with concrete *charis*, silver. Simonides' complaint about his empty money-box is consistent with the other anecdotes about the poet which stressed his acquisitiveness.[14] The point of this story hinges upon the interpretation of *charites*. Most commentators read "gratitude" or "thanks" for *charites* as the referent of the *charis* offered by the client and understand Simonides as grumbling because gratitude bears no purchasing power: What he really needs is money. One commentator is kinder to Simonides. In Austin's view, the poet has been promised *charis*, i.e., money, in return for a poem, but the money is not forthcoming. Simonides, pretending to misunderstand, replies that he has plenty of *charites* already (i.e., thanks), but no money.[15] But it is not the money container that is empty: the silver-coffer is described as "useful," and it is the coffer for *charites* which is "empty," "useless" (*kenên*).[16] Simonides cannot, then, mean "money" by his *charites*. He must mean more than "thanks," for he is not likely to be holding out for good manners: This would not be in keeping with the anecdotal tradition. The answer is to be found in Theocritus. Simonides, like the word play he inspired, is using *charites* to refer to his poems, in this case all sold (therefore the empty container). The *charis* (grateful response) offered by the client was empty, useless, because it was not backed up with money. Just so, Simonides' *charites* (poems) only appear when they are paid for; money is essential. The client will not get a *charis*-poem for his empty *charis*. Simonides requires prepayment.

Charites, in Dionysius Chalcus and Theocritus as in Si-

---

[14] These anecdotes were collected by Bell 1978, 29–86.

[15] Austin 1967, 11.

[16] The contrast is reinforced by the double occurrence of τὴν μὲν . . . τὴν δέ, first distinguishing two containers, then marking one as useless, one as useful. The two meanings of κενήν (5) may be significant here, as E. Robbins has observed (in private correspondence on this subject). If so, this expands even more the polyvalence of the punning. As "empty" the coffer for *charites* has no poems; as "useless" it may be full, but of (mere) thanks.

monides, referred to praise poems, tributes that were much sought after in a culture acutely sensitive to the deep pleasure that came with public acclaim. For this reason, the study of *charis* in archaic Greek poetry culminates in the epinician verses of Pindar and Bacchylides, where we find a complex tapestry woven from the variegated strands associated with *charis* in the poetry that preceded it. The glory, the *timê* that *charis* represented for the Homeric warrior, is translated into the awards that requite the effort expended by a winning athlete. The seductive beauty of Pandora becomes the transfigured beauty of the victor as he reaches the finish line ahead of his competitors; it also becomes the seductive and persuasive power of well-composed praise poetry. The social *charis*, *koinônia* experienced at the feast of Alcinous or the symposium, has a direct descendant in the victory feast of celebration. *Charis* in the lover's glance becomes the illuminating gaze of the admirers. The reciprocal benefits enjoyed by partners in a friendship or love relationship characterized by *charis* operate vigorously between poet and patron. The informal law of requital or *dikê* operates on all levels in the epinician sphere. *Charis* here as elsewhere exerts a civilizing influence, and in the world of kings, nobles, and legendary heroes who inform the verses of Bacchylides and Pindar, behaving without reciprocal *charis* and the mutual respect and kindness it requires is intolerable. The alliance of *charis* and the Charites with light-imagery produces a dazzling epiphany in epinician verse. The poets drink deeply of the association between joy or glory and illumination, and *charis* or the Charites not only highlight their chosen celebrand; they set him on fire. The cult of the Charites is a particularly rich store for associative language, particularly in Pindar, to whom the Orchomenian cult would be intimately known.

Chapter Six

EPINICIAN *CHARIS*

εὐκλέων δ' ἔργων ἄποινα χρὴ μὲν ὑμνῆσαι τὸν ἐσλόν,
χρὴ δὲ κωμάζοντ' ἀγαναῖς χαρίτεσσιν βαστάσαι.

As a reward for glorious deeds, one must sing praises of a
noble hero
And one must raise him high amid the *kômos*-festivities with
kindly *charites*.

Pindar *Isth.* 3.7–8

PINDAR'S song encompasses a *kômos*, the group of reveling celebrants who surrounded Melissus, a Theban athlete and victor in the chariot race at Nemea. After his victory and the glory that came with winning the victor's crown, there was still a necessary event, the performance of the song composed for the victory-party, a song that would "lift up" the victor and exalt his name. This was an act of commemoration that transcended time; the song could be repeated indefinitely. The power of praise poetry (here called "kindly *charites*") is clear. It can overcome the grievance of Archilochus that the *charis* of public respect and recognition is obliterated by death. This same claim was made on behalf of poetry by Theognis, Sappho, and Ibycus, as well as by Pindar and Bacchylides. Poets were the first to recognize the fact that the ultimate achievement of poetic *charis* was rescuing a mortal from mortality.[1]

---

[1] Theognis assures Cyrnus that, because of the glorifying gift of poetry, his memory will be kept alive as long as the sun shines over the earth (247–57). Ibycus makes a similar promise to Polycrates (fr. 282.46–48). Poetry rescues the poet as well as his or her subjects from oblivion. Sappho claims that she will live on after death because her poetry, of high quality and divinely inspired, will continue to be recited and praised (fr. 193). Pindar holds out the same hope for himself (*Pyth.* 3.110–12), and Bacchylides with

Without poetry, the *charis*-joy that comes from the fame of the moment will soon fade, says Pindar:

ἀλλὰ παλαιὰ γὰρ
εὕδει χάρις, ἀμνάμονες δὲ βροτοί,
ὅ τι μὴ σοφίας ἄωτον ἄκρον
κλυταῖς ἐπέων ῥοαῖσιν ἐξίκηται ζυγέν.

But the *charis* of long ago slumbers,
and mortals are unremembering,

of whatever does not arrive at the consummate bloom
of poetic composition, yoked to famous streams of words.

Pindar *Isth*. 7.16–19

Once again, it is the memory of the event that is crucial, if *charis* (here, the joy taken in successful achievement) is to remain awake and be constantly regenerated. Mortals forget, without a renewal of the original event in the repeated performances of the praise song. Such *charis* that will otherwise sleep is the pleasure awarded the celebrand by others; it consists in the admiration of the spectators at his victory celebration, but also of audiences who will see and hear the song performed in the future. Pindar contrasts with this the example of someone who has succeeded but whose successes have not been recorded in song: Commensurate with the short-lived public recollection of his achievement is his short-lived pleasure. Elsewhere, Pindar considers the victor who approaches death without commemoration in song. Such an athlete's aspirations and exertions are futile:

καὶ ὅταν καλὰ {μὲν} ἔρξαις ἀοιδᾶς ἄτερ,
'Αγησίδαμ', εἰς 'Αΐδα σταθμόν
ἀνὴρ ἵκηται, κενεὰ πνεύσαις ἔπορε μόχθῳ,
βραχύ τι τερπνόν.

---

quiet confidence links his own name with the immortalizing praise of Hieron at the end of his third epinician (95–97).

Whenever a man performs admirably, Hagesidamus,
without a song,
and he comes to the station of Hades,
he has toiled with aspirations that were hollow,
he has won a pleasure whose span was brief.

Pindar *Ol.* 10.91–93

Charis, then, in the epinician context, can represent the praise song itself or the public recognition that must be kept alive in song; but not to be forgotten is the fact that it represents the gratification of one man, the victor. Pindar mentions similar forms of *charis*-satisfaction: the sailor's pleasure at getting a following wind (*Pyth.* 1.33–34), the gratification of having one's prayer answered (*Isth.* 6.49–54), or the feeling of relief that comes with healing and the restoration of order after a period of instability (*Pyth.* 4.275). But, says Pindar, it is the *charis* of a good name that is the greatest possession:

<ἀλλ'> εἴ τις ἄκρον ἑλὼν
ἡσυχᾷ τε νεμόμενος αἰνὰν ὕβριν
ἀπέφυγεν, μέλανος {δ'} ἂν ἐσχατιὰν
καλλίονα θανάτου <στείχοι> γλυκυτάτᾳ γενεᾷ
εὐώνυμον κτεάνων κρατίσταν χάριν πορών.

(But) if someone had gained the summit
and, living in quiet, had avoided
dread arrogance, he would approach the furthest confines of
black death, which would appear all the fairer as he would be
passing on to his dear descendants
the *charis* of a good name, the mightiest of possessions.

Pindar *Pyth.* 11.55–58

As Pindar makes clear in the *Tenth Olympian* Ode (above), the final test comes at the moment of death: Have one's efforts and achievements in life transcended this blackness? Without a praise song, one's exertion in the competition will expire along with one's name. The tribute in song alone preserves this from becoming a hollow shade.

The praise poet, then, serves a vital role. The *charis* he provides represents gratification of the highest order in a society acutely sensitive to praise and blame. But the source of such *charis* lies outside society; it is ultimately a gift, a gift from the gods:

θεὸς ὁ πάντα τεύχων βροτοῖς
καὶ χάριν ἀοιδᾷ φυτεύει

It is the god who creates everything for mortals
and who begets *charis* in song.

Pindar fr. 141

Such a gift is not awarded gratuitously; the athlete's effort comes first. The wrestler Theaeus of Argos, says Pindar, can pray to Zeus for this divine favor, *charis*, and this prayer will be heard, for the athlete has done his part by demonstrating courage:

οὐδ' ἀμόχθῳ καρδίᾳ
προσφέρων τόλμαν παραιτεῖται χάριν.

And he prays for *charis*, contributing his own courage;
he does not do this with a heart that knows no toil.

Pindar *Nem.* 10.30–31

This divine gift, becoming immortalized in song—the gift of epinician *charis*—is not unlike the gilding of Odysseus. The Homeric hero had already proved his stature and followed divine instruction, and hence he had earned the favor of Athena: She poured *charis* over his beauty (*Od.* 6.235). Just so, rewarding the efforts of the victor and his trainer, the poet Pindar drips the gift of *charis*-delight over them both (*Isth.* 3/4.90–90b). The image of the poet's work as sprinkling, analogous to the divine gift of moisture that nourishes vegetation, appears in the *Tenth Olympian* Ode, where Pindar speaks of himself as sprinkling the victor while the Muses nourish his fame:

τὶν δ' ἁδυεπής τε λύρα
γλυκύς τ' αὐλὸς ἀναπάσσει χάριν·

τρέφοντι δ᾽ εὐρὺ κλέος
κόραι Πιερίδες Διός.

The honey-toned lyre and
the sweet pipe sprinkle you with *charis*
while the Muses, daughters of Zeus,
nourish a glory that spreads afar.

Pindar *Ol.* 10.93–96

Bacchylides, too, speaks of the Muse as "nurturing" the victor's glory. He assures Hieron that his distinction and the excellence that earned this, the ruler's *aretê*, will not be diminished in any way when he dies:

ἀρετᾶ[ς γε μ]ὲν οὐ μινύθει
βροτῶν ἅμα σ[ώμ]ατι φέγγος, ἀλλὰ
Μοῦσά νιν τρ[έφει.]

The light of mortals' distinction does not wane
at the same time as does their body, but
the Muse nurtures it.

Bacchylides 3.90–92

The divine power Pindar speaks of exercising in partnership with the Muses, that of bringing into being, of nursing or fostering growth, is clearly tied to a belief in the gods' creative power through the giving of moisture, but there is more to be derived from the specific image of sprinkling. An athlete was proclaimed winner in the games at the moment when he was presented with a leafy garland (see Fig. 4). The signaling of congratulation by crowning someone with lush greenery has its roots in the *phyllobolia*, the custom of throwing leaves at one who was enjoying good fortune.[2] When

---

[2] On the *phyllobolia* see Jebb 1905 *ad* 10.17–20; Nisetich 1975, 59n.17; Brown 1990, 184–86; and Hollis 1990, 222–23. For the custom of *phyllobolia* as operative in the passage taken from *Ol.* 10, see Verdenius 1987 *ad* 94 s.v. ἀναπάσσει. Pindar himself gives the prototype for athletic contexts in his description of a Cyrenaean bride-race. The first in the race to touch the robes of the Libyan princess secures his bride and is showered with garlands and leaves (*Pyth.* 9.123–125). With this may be compared the wedding procession of Helen and Menelaus, as described by Stesichorus (fr.

FIGURE 4. *Victorious athlete*, on a Protolucanian *pelikê*, fifth century B.C.E. A victor receives his awards, including a leaf garland presented by the woman on the right.

Pindar describes the epiphany of Alcmaeon (*Pyth.* 8.57–60), he pictures himself as covering the hero with garlands and sprinkling him with song.

Garlands, wreaths and flowers were presented to a fortunate few, not as tokens of wealth but as signs of life flourishing. Wreaths were worn by guests at a symposium or by participants in a *kômos*, festive events that celebrated the vigor and pleasure of collective life.[3] The lushness of the leaves that crowned the head of the athlete was on a continuum with his proven physical strength that demonstrated life at its prime. This was the domain of Thalia.

Another epinician image related to sprinkling with green vegetation is that of weaving, and in this the Charites are involved. Bacchylides commemorates Hieron's first victory at Olympia in 476 B.C.E., describing his task as "weaving a song with the Charites:"

ἤ σὺν Χαρίτεσσι βαθυζώνοις ὑφάνας
    ὕμνον ἀπὸ ζαθέας
νάσου ξένος ὑμετέραν
    ἐς κλυτὰν πέμπει πόλιν

---

187). The bride is showered with quinces, myrtle leaves, garlands of roses, and violets. The custom persists, of course, with our tossing confetti.

[3] See Blech 1982, 63–65. Collective life was nowhere more vigorously celebrated than at the symposium. The dithyrambic poet Philoxenus (early fourth century B.C.E.) in his *Symposium* described the presentation of the myrtle wreath, along with the ritual cleansing of hands, as signaling the beginning of the festivities. The language is reminiscent of the lush delicacy of Sappho's poetry:

. . . ἁπαλὸς παιδίσκος . . .
εἶτ᾿ ἔφερεν στέφανον λεπτᾶς ἀπὸ μυρτίδος
εὐγνήτων κλάδων δισύναπτον.

Then a tender boy
brought a garland made of delicate myrtle
from vigorous branches, double-plaited.

Philoxenus, fr. 836 *PMG*

The wreaths are fresh, lush, and pliant like the young boy, expressing the continuum between human and natural growth reflected in the *phyllobolia*.

Weaving a song with the deep-girdled Charites,
a guest-friend sends you a song from a hallowed isle
to your famous city

Bacchylides 5.9–12

In what sense can Bacchylides be thinking of his poetic craft as weaving? The Charites were feminine, and the image could call to mind the traditional stance of women in front of their loom.[4] The poet, with the Charites at his side, is weaving poetic threads into an intricate poetic fabric. The physical structure of the loom and the lyre were similar, and the association was natural. Weaving involved design and the imposition of order; as early as Homer, weaving was used as a metaphor for intellectual activity.[5] Occasionally, Pindar's references to weaving songs derive from the activity of weaving garments. The poet is weaving variegated material into one beautiful and complex whole (e.g., *Ol.* 6.86–87). But the Charites were not normally introduced as divine counterparts of Greek housewives at their domestic chores, and their presence here, along with Bacchylides' epithet "deep-girdled" (9), suggests that the goddesses are adding beauty to the poet's song. Pindar, in the *Ninth Pythian* Ode, also speaks of his having composed a song with the "deep-girdled Charites":

Ἐθέλω χαλκάσπιδα Πυθιονίκαν
σὺν βαθυζώνοισιν ἀγγέλλων
Τελεσικράτη Χαρίτεσσι γεγωνεῖν
ὄλβιον ἄνδρα διωξίππου στεφάνωμα Κυράνας·

---

[4] Another triad of divine women weave, of course—the Fates. One of them, Clôthô, shared a name with the verb "to spin" (κλώθω) and, even more importantly for this context, "a wreath" (κλωθώ).

[5] See Maehler 1982 *ad* 5.9, and Snyder 1981, 193–96. Snyder gives examples of the Homeric use of weaving to represent intellectual activity and points out the structural similarity between the loom and the lyre. Weaving as a metaphor for poetry making is also attested in Old English (*wordcræft [e] wæf*; Cynewulf, *Elene* 1238), so that the metaphor is said to date back to Indo-European (Schmitt 1967, 300). I am grateful to Marta Steele for this reference.

I wish to shout aloud as I proclaim
with the deep-girdled Charites that
Telesicrates is the man, Pythian victor with the bronze shield,
blessed, the crowning garland of chariot-driving Cyrene.

Pindar *Pyth.* 9.1–4

The words "with the deep-girdled Charites" may be a
direct echo of the phrase in the fifth ode of Bacchylides,
written two years earlier,[6] but it is the connection with a
garland (4) which is interesting. The athlete Telesicrates *is* a
garland: He crowns his city as he himself was crowned in
the games. The epinician poet then performs a third and
climactic crowning with his song-garland.[7] The culmination
is extended by the repetition of the ode, a perpetual coronation. Why are the Charites present in this context? Because
they carry echoes of lush fecundity from their early presentation as vegetation goddesses, and this echo enhances the
imagery of the garland crown.

Bacchylides presses the wreath-garland allusion to the
Charites in his dithyramb for Athens:

Πάρεστι μυρία κέλευθος
    ἀμβροσίων μελέων,
ὃς ἂν παρὰ Πιερίδων λά-
    χῃσι δῶρα Μουσᾶν,
ἰοβλέφαροί τε κ<όρ>αι
    φερεστέφανοι Χάριτες
    βάλωσιν ἀμφὶ τιμάν

---

[6] Jebb 1905 *ad* Bacch. 5.9 ff. suggests this. But the same combination of
garlands, a poem, and the Charites occurs at the end of Pindar's *Fifth
Nemean* Ode (53–54), an ode composed much earlier than were the *Ninth
Pythian* or Bacchylides 5.

[7] In several of his odes, Pindar's weaving imagery permits him to speak
of himself as an active participant in the victory. In the *Seventh Nemean* Ode,
he describes his poetic composition in various metaphors drawn from the
pentathlon, culminating in his making a wreath (77). In his *Third Olympian*,
he describes himself as wearing a wreath, thus prompted to compose a
song (6–7).

ὕμνοισιν· ὕφαινέ νῦν ἐν
 ταῖς πολυηράτοις τι καινὸν
 ὀλβίαις Ἀθάναις
 εὐαίνετε Κηΐα μέριμνα.

There are at hand many paths of immortal songs
for one who takes his gifts from the Pierian Muses,
and the dark-eyed maidens, garland-bearing Charites
crown with honor
the festive odes.[8] Weave now,
O much-praised attentiveness from Ceos,
some fresh composition
for Athens, most lovely, blessed.

Bacchylides 19.1–11

Here the Charites crown the poet's songs just as in cult they would celebrate a god, a hero, or the revered dead by a coronation of wreaths.[9]

The *charis* of song, the poet's coronation of the victor, brings into the epinician context the life-enhancing powers of the Charites. When Pindar composes a victory-ode for the Syracusan despot Hieron, winner in the Pythian horse-races of 482 and 478 B.C.E. but in failing health, he speaks of himself as wishing he could send Hieron "twin-*charites*":

τῷ μὲν διδύμας χάριτας
 εἰ κατέβαν ὑγίειαν ἄγων χρυσέαν
  κῶμόν τ᾽ ἀέθλων Πυθίων αἴγλαν στεφάνοις

If I could have come to him bringing
twin-*charites*, golden health
and the victory song, a radiant gleam
added to the wreaths of those Pythian games

Pindar *Pyth*. 3.72–73

[8] Lit. "cast honor around the praise songs." The image is once again one of crowning; the poet's songs are garlanded, just as the songs themselves were wreaths for the victors. On the crowning metaphor in the epinician context, see Nisetich 1975, 55–68.

[9] For example, on the relief from Thasos (above, Ch. 3, n.11), where the three women (Charites?) are in a linear procession with Apollo, Hermes, and nymphs, carrying garlands. One of them appears to be about to crown Hermes.

The poem is, as E. Robbins has recently pointed out, strongly consolatory in tone. [10] The focus is on Hieron's two great desires—restored health and a victory celebration—desires that Pindar wishes he could fulfil; gratification of these desires would be satisfaction of the most intense order, hence *charites*. Hieron was suffering from acute pain[11] and was confronted with his own mortality as well as, in all likelihood, a recent defeat in the games at Delphi. The wished-for transformation from sorrow to joy, ultimately a divine gift and not in Pindar's power to bestow, the poet calls a *charis*, in the myth contained in the second part of the ode. According to the myth, the royal house of Thebes, after suffering great adversity, changed their condition and "set their hearts aright." This reversal is a "*charis* of Zeus." The turnabout action on the part of the house of Thebes was impossible without divine intervention:

Διὸς δὲ χάριν
ἐκ προτέρων μεταμειψάμενοι καμάτων
ἔστασαν ὀρθὰν καρδίαν.

A *charis* of Zeus,[12]
they raised a heart that was upright, turning
from their former tribulations.

Pindar Pyth. 3.95–96

Pindar could not offer Hieron twin-*charites*, i.e., a complete release from his troubles, which would be parallel to the *charis* provided for Thebes by Zeus. But if he could not hold out to the despot the hope of physical immortality, still he could offer hope of another sort. The preservation of Hieron's name and fame in song, like the celebration of the heroes in Homeric epic, was within the poet's power to confer. Ajax with his blood-stained body brought shame

---

[10] Robbins 1990a, 307–18. My interpretation of this ode is heavily indebted to this article.

[11] He suffered from the stone and had to be carried on a litter (see Farnell 1932 *ad Pyth.* 1.47–57).

[12] This reading takes χάριν in apposition to the phrase ἔστασαν ὀρθὰν καρδίαν. See Appendix 2.

upon the Greeks by his suicide, but the verses of Homer transformed his act until he was honored throughout the world (*Isth*. 4.37–41). Poetry transforms the ugly into the beautiful, the dying into the living. This is the *charis* of the poet's power, and it gleams. Beautiful deeds well described in verse become a ray of light shining over earth and sea, unquenchable (*Isth*. 4.45–46). The timeless praise of the victory ode reflected upon the poet as well. The praise poets linked their own fame with that of the victors they celebrated. Their reputation would be coeval, a *charis* for both. Bacchylides does not pass up the opportunity to share in the greatest victory of Hieron's career:

Ἱέρων, σὺ δ᾽ ὄλβου
κάλλιστ᾽ ἐπεδ[είξ]αο θνατοῖς
ἄνθεα· πράξα[ντι] δ᾽ εὖ
οὐ φέρει κόσμ[ον σι]ω-
πά· σὺν δ᾽ ἀλαθ[είᾳ] καλῶν
καὶ μελιγλώσσου τις ὑμνήσει χάριν
Κηίας ἀηδόνος.

Hieron, you demonstrated to mortals
the fairest flower, blessedness.
For one who has performed well,
silence is not becoming.
Along with the true record of your fair deeds,
one will sing praises as well of the *charis*
of the honey-voiced nightingale of Ceos.

Bacchylides 3.92–98

Hieron commissioned this ode from Bacchylides to celebrate his victory in the chariot race at Olympia in 468 B.C.E., the culmination of his racing career. It was no less a triumph for Bacchylides, who received the commission in preference to Pindar. The double distinction for patron and poet is alluded to with dextrous ambiguity in the above verses, the closing epode of this poem.[13] As they sing the record of

---

[13] The χάρις of v.97 has given rise to several interpretations and has

Hieron's great accomplishment, people will be singing praises of the song itself. The fact that Bacchylides frames *charis* (*charin*, 97) with words applying the praise to himself makes it clear that the glorification contained in this *charis*-song belongs to both men.

The same discreet combination of poetic tributes is found in Bacchylides' dithyramb for Athens (Bacchylides 19, above), here he refers to himself as "much-praised attentiveness from Ceos" (11), praising the victor, but he refers to his songs as garlanded with honor by the Charites, replicating the victor's crowning with his wreath. Pindar is less cautious. In the *Third Pythian* Ode (110–15), he concludes his

---

been translated variously as the "charm" of the poet (see the bibliography in Maehler 1982 *ad loc.*), his "song" (Fränkel 1975, 464n.44), the "charm" of the song (Gerber 1984 s.v. χάρις and Lomiento 1990, 123), or a complex including all of these (Burnett 1985, 76). χάριν has also been taken as a quasi-preposition, giving the following translation for vv. 97–98: "there shall be a song of praise . . . and by grace also of the honey-voiced nightingale of Ceos" (Woodbury 1969, 331–35). This interpretation leaves ὑμνήσει, normally transitive, without an expressed object (although see Woodbury's n.12, 334).

It is, I think, preferable to retain the full powers of χάριν as a noun, allowing it to represent at this climactic moment in the ode the pleasure and the power conferred by this song, on Hieron but no less on the gifted poet from Ceos. This is the view of Maehler (1982 *ad* 96–98): "Die Gedankenreihe 'Hieron ist gesegnet—den Erfolgreichen muß man preisen' kulminiert in dem Satz 'Man wird das Lied singen.'" Maehler points out that the gesture of the poet (i.e., the χάρις, his song), following up Hieron's successes, is analogous to the thought contained in the earlier part of the conclusion, where the Muse nurtures success (72). In his comments on 97 (τις ὑμνήσει χάριν) Maehler points out another structural advantage of this interpretation, which takes χάρις as a noun: ὑμνήσει recalls the ὕμνει of the proem (3) and μελίγλωσσος together with the χάρις (the poet's gift) picks up the reference to the Muse-with-sweet-gift, γλυκύδωρε Κλεοῖ, also from v. 3. In a kind of ring-composition, the ode opens and closes with the idea of singing the sweet gifts of poetry. Maehler sees Bacchylides' syntax as a display of self-praise that is far from discreet: The phrase σὺν δ᾽ ἀλαθείᾳ καλῶν, he says, while a reference to the praise-poem's glorification of Hieron, prepares the way for, hence is secondary to, what follows, the *charis* (song) tribute to the poet. In translating the χάρις of 97, we can scarcely do better than "praise song."

great tribute to Hieron with an acknowledgment of his own aspirations for wealth and towering fame. In doing so he associates himself with with Nestor and Sarpedon, heroes among the select few who earned their fame through being preserved in poetry.[14]

Bacchylides, in his third ode, described his song as an *alatheia* of Hieron's performance (96). *Alatheia*, like *charis*, is a complex notion in praise poetry and, like *charis*, it lies at the core of the epinician experience. At the opening of the *Eighth Olympian* Ode, Pindar addresses Olympia, site of the games first founded in 776 B.C.E., as "queen of *alatheia*." In what way can a racecourse be said to be the monarch of truth? The answer lies in a different understanding of truth from our own. The games were the proving ground for young athletes, the touchstone that revealed them as "true" winners or losers. The idea of truth as revelation, particularly in the sense of "non-overlooking," is contained in the word *alatheia*.[15] The praise-poems scrutinized, then revealed, this "truth" of victorious performance, at a secondary and more permanent stage of the victory celebration, much as they duplicated the crowning of the victors. Rescuing this moment from oblivion, the poet's role was crucial. In his eighth ode, Bacchylides takes an oath to praise "with *alatheia*" when the whole event can shine forth in the light of public disclosure:

κομπάσομαι· σὺν ἀλα-
θείᾳ δὲ πᾶν λάμπει χρέος·

I will make this boast; and with *alatheia* all comes to light.

Bacchylides 8.20

---

[14] The same undisguised hopes conclude the *First Olympian*, where he expresses the desire to continue consorting with victors all his life, so that he can be "far-famed for (his) poetry" (116).

[15] The etymological connection between *alatheia* and ἀ-λανθάνω, ἀ-λήθη, would appear to have been consciously present in the use of the word in early Greek literature (Maehler 1982 *ad* Bacchylides 3.96). For discussions of *alatheia* in early Greek thought, see the following: Woodbury 1969, 333 and n.10; Komornicka 1972, 235–53; Kahn 1973, 363–66; Levet 1976, 78–105; Gentili 1981, 215–20; and Cole 1983, 7–28.

The illumination brought about by the poet's work "with *alatheia*" consists of a rescue from the darkness of forgetfulness (*lêthê*), then a perpetual glorification. In fr. 205, Pindar addresses *Alatheia* as a queen, calling her the origin of *aretê* (great deeds of excellence) and directing her to guide him accordingly:

'Αρχὰ μεγάλας ἀρετᾶς
ὤνασσ' 'Αλάθεια, μὴ πταίσῃς ἐμάν
σύνθεσιν τραχεῖ ποτὶ ψεύδει

Origin of mighty excellence
Queen *Alatheia*, don't cause my commission
to stumble over brute falsehood

Pindar fr. 205

Pindar gives us here a clear statement of his professional responsibility when under contract.[16] As *alatheia* served the sovereign Olympia in proving/revealing victors (*Ol.* 8.1–2), so the poet serves the queen *Alatheia* in giving an accurate testimony of the victory event. In his fifth ode, Bacchylides speaks of his responsibility to praise as a *charis* of *alatheia*:

χρὴ] δ' ἀλαθείας χάριν
αἰνεῖν, φθόνον ἀμφ[οτέραισιν
χερσὶν ἀπωσάμενον,
εἰ τις εὖ πράσσοι βροτῶ[ν.

One must praise, a *charis* of *alatheia*,
Keeping envy at bay with both hands,
If some mortal should perform well.

Bacchylides 5.187–90

Taking the *charin* of v. 187 as a noun in apposition to the verb of praising,[17] the poet's praise becomes a pleasure-bestowing service of *alatheia*, inasmuch as it gives a perma-

---

[16] See Gentili 1981, 219–20, who calls this a statement of Pindar's professional ethic. σύνθεσις, like the συνθέμενος of *Nem.* 4.74, refers to the poet's commission for celebrating the victory. Pindar's homage to Alatheia reflects his respect for the relation between poet and patron, the reciprocal advantage of which will occur with a revelation by the poem.

[17] It is so taken by Fränkel 1975, 128n.26. See Appendix 2.

nent commemoration of the outstanding performance. A poetic record that followed this course was a pledge:

εἰ δὲ σὺν πόνῳ τις εὖ πράσσοι, μελιγάρυες ὕμνοι
ὑστέρων ἀρχὰ λόγων
τέλλεται[18] καὶ πιστὸν ὅρκιον μεγάλαις ἀρεταῖς·

If someone should perform well with exertion, honey-voiced songs arise as the origin for fame in future years
and they are a faithful pledge in return for mighty excellence.

Pindar Ol. 11.4–6

The linguistic resemblances between this passage and Pindar's fr. 205 (above) are striking. *Alatheia* is the "origin of mighty deeds" in fr. 205 and praise songs are the "origin of fame" and the "pledge of mighty deeds" in *Ol.* 11. As "origins," praise songs with their *alatheia* have a creative power. They launch the immortalizing process of poetry. What was present in potential at the moment of trial in the games is only given actualized form when the poet records it for posterity. This duplication of the epinician event, with the teleological force of the praise song, led the poets to use such descriptions as "legitimately begotten" to describe the songs. In Bacchylides' ninth ode, the victory "wins songs engendered of itself" (83). The feat of the victory performance becomes the legitimate parent of the song that continues to sing its praise long after the parent is dead.

The formative power of the poet's record is only possible, however, because the songs are composed with the pleasure-bearing component of *charis* or the Charites, as well as with an accurate testimony of the winning performance. Bacchylides in his nineteenth ode (above) draws upon the Muses, daughters of Mnemosyne (Memory), for confirmation of the accuracy of his report but confesses an additional need for the "deep-girdled Charites." Only by making the song beautiful will the poet make it attractive to future gen-

---

[18] The singular verb τέλλεται is accounted for by attraction to the predicate ἀρχά. For the construction see Verdenius 1988 *ad loc.*

erations outliving the single performance. At the opening of his *Fourth Nemean* Ode, Pindar describes the joy (*euphrosynê*) attendant upon winning in the games. He speaks of this joy as a "healer" and specifically ties it to the soothing effects of songs that record the victory. The songs he calls "daughters of the Muses" and he speaks of his conscious effort to extract his material after deep reflection. The Muses will provide the substance for his poetry, but it is the Charites who will ensure that the word outlives the deeds:

ῥῆμα δ᾽ ἐργμάτων χρονιώτερον βιοτεύει,
ὅ τι κε σὺν Χαρίτων τύχᾳ
γλῶσσα φρενὸς ἐξέλοι βαθείας.

The word lives longer than the deeds,
Whatever it is that the tongue draws up, taking
draughts from deep in the mind,
With the good fortune of the Charites' presence.

Pindar Nem. 4.6–9

This complementary function of the Muses and Charites is also expressed in metaphor. In the *Sixth Nemean* Ode, Pindar speaks of the Muses as providing him with fertile fields to till (32). It is the Charites, however, who nourish the beautiful growth that emerges from the soil and assure its excellence: They give the poet a "choice flower" (*Isth.* 8.17) from a "choice garden" (*Ol.* 9.27).[19]

Pindar's effort to maintain an allegiance to a faithful record of the event he commemorates he describes as "drinking deeply from the depths of his mind." This, like the "faithful pledge" of *Ol.* 11.6 or Bacchylides' "much-praised attentiveness from Ceos" (19.11), are indications that the poets felt bound to take their commissions seriously. Pindar

---

[19] Verdenius, in his commentary on Pindar's *Fourteenth Olympian*, 1987, 105, writes: "(Pindar) feels inspired by the Muses, who as daughters of Mnemosyne, determine the factual contents of a poem . . . and the Charites, who determine the effect on the audience." (For Pindaric passages where there is a close connection between the Muses and the Charites, see his n.6.)

speaks of his patron as "laboring for his *charis*" (*Pyth*. 10.64). The visible form this took was no doubt that of financial remuneration, but Pindar's description of his patron relationship as one of *xenia* or *philia* as well as *charis* suggests that it provided mutual benefit. His patrons he calls *xeinoi* (guest-friends); he is their *philos* (friend). The praise poet abided by the reciprocal laws of friendship and guest exchange. This reciprocity was so marked that the distinctions between donor and recipient were virtually dissolved.[20] Pindar refers to this fusion with a remarkable expression: In supplying the commission the patron is yoking the chariot of the Muses, "eagerly loving one who loves, and leading one who leads" (*Pyth*. 10.65).

In a similar way, the poet and athlete participated in a common experience, the one event that would reward the labors of both with fame. Pindar's mind drifts to this pleasurable moment:

εἴ τί τοι Πίσας τε καὶ Φερενίκου χάρις
νόον ὑπὸ γλυκυτάταις ἔθηκε φροντίσιν

If in some way the *charis* of the (games at) Pisa and of (the horse) Pherenicus
has placed (my) mind in the midst of sweetest thoughts.

Pindar *Ol*. 1.18–19

Not only was the production of victory songs gratifying for the poet, earning him a rightful place among the nobility in his world (*Ol*. 1.115–16, *Pyth*. 2.96–97),[21] but he stood to gain lasting admiration for his work. Sometimes this even came during his lifetime, once from an entire state (*Pyth*. 1.75–79).

[20] On the deliberate ambiguity Pindar produced by these reciprocal references to poet and patron, an expression of the bond between members of the nobility, see Crotty 1982, 79.

[21] On the degree to which Pindar's world was contained within the confines of the aristocracy, see Kurke 1991, 92–156. She demonstrates the ways in which aristocratic conventions such as gift exchange or other actions that conferred prestige—"top-rank occasions"—informed Pindar's metaphors for the epinician process.

The song of commemoration is frequently described as a "necessary," "needed," or "fitting" follow-up to the victory. The performance called for a poetic requital. This vocabulary of self-reference by the epinician poets, who speak of their work as requital, has been the subject of the formalistic literary study of Pindar done by E. L. Bundy.[22] L. Kurke argues that this poetic motif is drawn from the activities of an aristocratic community that depended upon mutual praise and conferring of prestige to forestall agonistic disintegration. The athlete's performance, which incurred a "loss" to himself with his outlay of expense and effort, threatened the communal balance, and recompense was necessary.[23]

In fact, the victory celebration consisted of a requital complex on several levels, when the victor and his community basked in the pleasure of shared glory. The celebration where the ode would be sung was more intimate than the initial triumph before the larger assembly of spectators. Being more intimate, it reflected bonds that were more personal, gratification that went deeper and was the appropriate milieu in which to find *charis*. The victory-*kômos* in the athlete's hometown, the communal feasting, and the performance of the victory song were direct descendants of that feast of Alcinous described by Odysseus as a "fulfilment full of *charis*" (*Od.* 9.5). The acclaim that the victor received he awarded in turn to his city, his kin, his trainer, and even his deceased ancestors. Pindar speaks of the city's thirst for glory, which is quenched by the victory (*Nem.* 5.47); this

---

[22] 1962. Bundy calls this literary convention the "χρέος-motive" (see, for example, I.10–12, 21–22, and II.57, 67, 85) and characterizes what he calls the "necessity or propriety that determines the relationship between song and merit" (I.10–11) as the fulfilment of desire. χάρις is the appropriate word for this context: The merit "desires" the song that "desires" the merit/victory. For a discussion of the song as "fitting," and the way in which Pindar's metaphors are not empty but infused with cultural practices, see Gundert 1935, 125n.195. For the inner connection between victory and song, see Schadewaldt 1928a, 277n.1, and Woodbury 1968, 527–42, who discusses the role of the poet's contract and how this colors Pindar's language of requital.

[23] Kurke 1991, 108–17.

satisfied the agonistic drive of Greek cities to be able to claim one of their own as victor, and all the townspeople fully participated in this *charis*-joy:

'Ερατιδᾶν τοι σὺν χαρίτεσσιν ἔχει
θαλίας καὶ πόλις·

With the *charites* of the clan of the Eratidae
the city too has its festivities.

Pindar Ol. 7.93–94

The plural word *charites* here, reinforced by the word *thaliai*, suggests that Pindar was thinking of the town as flourishing under the patronage of the Charites at this moment. Thalia, who nourishes festivity, gave her name (in the plural form) to festive occasions. In another Pindaric ode, the *charis* of the celebration-party is likened to funeral rites of libation that renew the dead, like giving water to living plants. An epinician offering can be made to the dead, renewing their link with the living. Together they are bound in "communal *charis*":[24]

μεγαλᾶν δ' ἀρετᾶν
δρόσῳ μαλθακᾷ
ῥανθεισᾶν κώμων {θ'} ὑπὸ χεύμασιν,
ἀκούοντί ποι χθονίᾳ φρενί,
σφὸν ὄλβον υἱῷ τε κοινὰν χάριν
ἔνδικόν τ' Ἀρκεσίλᾳ·

Somehow they hear, with their underworldly spirit,
of the actions of great prowess,
sprinkled with soft dew
beneath the outpourings of the festive bands;
this is their own blessing,
and the *charis*[25] they share with their son,
the rightful due of Arcesilaus.

Pindar Pyth. 5.98–103

---

[24] The following text is taken from the Oxford edition by Bowra 1947. The reason for replacing the edition of Snell-Maehler in this instance is given in the following note.

[25] This reading takes χάριν in apposition to the foregoing phrase, like

Like Odysseus making a blood offering to the shades in *Odyssey* 11 so that he can communicate with them, the victory *kômos* pours out a stream of song, so that the dead ancestors of Arcesilaus can share in the *charis* of the victory celebration.

In the *Eighth Olympian* Ode, Pindar's ritual language is slightly different but the effect is the same. The victor can share a portion of the *charis* with the members of his family who have died because the whole event is a type of rite:

ἔστι δὲ καί τι θανόντεσσιν μέρος
κὰν νόμον ἐρδομένων·
κατακρύπτει δ' οὐ κόνις

συγγόνων κεδνὰν χάριν.

Yes, there is even some share for the dead
in the due performance of the rite;
dust does not cover up
the cherished *charis* of one's kin.

Pindar Ol. 8.77–80

The young, in winning a victory and participating in a communal celebration, were performing a *nomos*, a "convention" that, like a sacrificial ritual, sustained the community as a group.[26] The victory was a deep-rooted aspiration common to everyone; attaining it was a success for all. The bond between the members, living and dead,[27] was renewed, much as recounting the great deeds of dead heroes and ancestors would revive their sense of commonality.[28]

---

the Διὸς χάριν of *Pyth.* 3.95 (cited above). My preference is for the (accusative) μεγάλαν δ' ἀρετὰν (Bowra 1947) over the (genitive) μεγαλᾶν δ' ἀρετᾶν (Snell-Maehler 1987). Both are of course possible after the verb ἀκούοντι but the accusatives are a more natural antecedent for χάριν and ὄλβον.

[26] Gildersleeve 1890 *ad loc.* compares this use of *nomos* to Hesiod's *Theog.* 416.

[27] This bond is ritual in nature, and different from the active, mutually satisfying bond between living members of a community, whose disappearance at birth Archilochus laments (Ch. 5 above).

[28] Cf. Pindar's *Pyth.* 9.93, where winning in the games is described as an experience "well-toiled for the common good" (ἐν ξυνῷ πεπονᾱμένον εὖ).

The performance of the praise song was no more a private event than was a victory in the games. Pindar describes his role as one who was "dispatched, an individual sent on behalf of the community" (*Ol.* 13.49). His message was one for all, touching everyone (*Ol.* 7.21), repaying a single athlete but at the same time bringing *charis*-joy to all:

κοινὸν λόγον
φίλαν τείσομεν ἐς χάριν.

We will pay up the account in which all have a share,
for a *charis* of friendship.

Pindar *Ol.* 10.11–12

Pindar's use of the verb *tinein* ("to repay," "to avenge," v. 12) is significant.[29] The poet, by satisfying his commission and paying an (encomiastic) indemnity to the athlete, restores the balance, much as giving Achilles his due honors would redress an imbalance created by his being shamed. This restoration of the general social equilibrium by paying the dues owed to an individual member of the community means that the joy is at once private and communal.[30]

For the importance of the athletic events as *paideia*, see Gundert 1935, 32n.1.

[29] The word ἄποινα, which Pindar often uses in this context to refer to the poet's recompense for the victor, is actually an intensive form of ποινή ("penalty"), as Robbins 1990, 12n.33, points out. Robbins makes the important point that with ποινή and τιμή coming from the same Indo-European root, "there is a profound and important connection between the two ideas: Restitution or indemnity (τιμή) is a form of satisfaction in a carefully calibrated exchange system whose satisfactions include penalties, ransom, and honor."

[30] On the public nature of the poem, therefore its public benefit, see Kurke 1991, 101–2, who speaks of the victor as putting the whole aristocratic community in his debt until the poet's act of release. With his poem, Pindar reconstitutes the community. Pindar's role is a complex one. On one level, he is simply satisfying a commission, a contract between him and his patron. But on another level he is participating in the larger social scheme, where he accepts responsibility for the well-being of an entire community. On this level, the strength of his obligation is greater, even though his choice to undertake it was a free one. The bonding between members of the community was established by a *charis* that is at once a free and an obligatory service. On this see Schadewaldt 1928, 277n.2, and Gundert 1935, 32.

The private joy that belonged to the athlete began with the victory. Pindar speaks of it as "sweet recompense" (*Nem.* 5.48) or as a "breathing-space from exertions" (*Ol.* 8.7). The pleasure of this release from effort, which was, in addition, a reward, meant that *charis* was used to represent victory when it was expressed as some form of requital for effort.[31] But effort was not the only thing requited. The athletes were rewarded for their piety as much as for their prowess:

τῶν δὲ μόχθων ἀμπνοάν.
ἄνεται δὲ πρὸς χάριν εὐσεβίας ἀνδρῶν λιταῖς·

. . . a breathing-space from their toils.
It comes about through the prayers of men, in answer
to the *charis* of their piety.

Pindar Ol. 8.7–8

The *charis* of the athletes' prayers pleases the gods, so divine response can be expected. The public acclaim that the athletes received Pindar describes as coming from *aidoia Charis*, a divine Charis that possesses and claims *aidôs*. The beauty conferred by this Charis amounts to a physical transformation of the victor, but, with the *aidôs* coming from a divine figure, the act becomes a beatification as well as a beautification:

αἰδοία ποτιστά-
ξῃ Χάρις εὐκλέα μορφάν.

Charis that claims *aidôs*
distills over him a glorifying figure.

Pindar Ol. 6.76

The divine combination of *charis* and *aidôs* and the awe it inspires recalls the encounter between Demeter and Metaneira. As Metaneira was taken aback by the strange and overbearing presence so, says Pindar (praying to Zeus on behalf of a victorious athlete), may even strangers be

---

[31] On the connection between χάρις and such words as λύτρον (release) or ἄποινα (compensation) see Schadewaldt 1928a, 277, and 278n.1.

touched with the *charis* of the athlete which possesses and claims *aidôs*:

δίδοι τέ οἱ αἰδοίαν χάριν
καὶ ποτ᾽ ἀστῶν καὶ ποτὶ ξεί-
νων.

May (Zeus) grant him the *charis* of *aidôs*
from his townspeople and from visitors alike.

Pindar *Ol.* 7.89–90

The divine power of Charis distilled beauty on the victor. This made him as alluring as he was awe-inspiring, like Odysseus on the shore attracting the attention of Nausicaa after his *charis*-unction. Young women watching the athletic event look at the successful athlete and long to have such a man for a husband (*Pyth.* 9.98–99).[32]

The divinized Charis appears again in Pindar, in his *Seventh Olympian* Ode, with the powerful epithet *zôthalmios* (life-flourishing). This Charis, in which the features of Thalia predominate, looks upon the victor with favor:

ὁ δ᾽ ὄλβιος, ὃν φᾶμαι κατέχωντ᾽ ἀγαθαί·
ἄλλοτε δ᾽ ἄλλον ἐποπτεύ-
ει Χάρις ζωθάλμιος ἁδυμελεῖ
θαμὰ μὲν φόρμιγγι παμφώνοισί τ᾽ ἐν ἔντεσιν αὐλῶν.

Blessed is he to whom good report attaches itself.
Charis of life-flourishing power looks with favor upon one at one time, another at another,
with the repeated chords of the sweet-sounding lyre
and the wide-ranging notes of the pipes.

Ol. 7.10–12

Indeed, the powers of Thalia infuse the entire poem. The birth and growth of the island of Rhodes (69–70) with its vegetative imagery underscores the continuum of nature which, in the poetry of Pindar, penetrates all aspects of

---

[32] The effect of the physical transformation by χάρις is akin to that of Sappho's bridegroom in fr. 112, honored by Aphrodite with a χάριεν εἶδος.

human experience.[33] The nuptial wine-bowl, the *charis*[34] that opens the ode, has symbolic powers to perpetuate new growth through a marriage. These are parallel to the fecundating powers of the poet, who sends the victor "liquid nectar," the "sweet fruit" of his powers of composition (7–8). With this we can compare the poet's power described in the *Ninth Nemean* Ode. Here he makes the victor's fame "filled with new *thalia*" (*neothalês*, v. 48). Again, the second formative event of the praise poem repeats, recasts, regenerates the prior event, imitating a process drawn from nature.

The song-garland woven by Pindar and Bacchylides was another of these second, formative events, a second coronation in which the Thalia aspect of the Charites was predominant. As there was no distinction to be made between nature's growth and human flourishing, so could the poets view the fecundity of their powers of composition as deriving from the work of Thalia and the Charites. Pindar speaks of himself as harvesting delights from the garden of the Charites:

ἐξαίρετον Χαρίτων νέμομαι κᾶπον·
κεῖναι γὰρ ὤπασαν τὰ τέρπν'· ἀγαθοὶ
    δὲ καὶ σοφοὶ κατὰ δαίμον' ἄνδρες
ἐγένοντ'·

---

[33] On the unity of nature and its celebration in the poetry of Pindar, see Duchemin 1965, 249n.26. Young 1968, 97, says of Pindar's description of the "new growth" of Rhodes in this poem, along with the collocation of Χάριτες and θαλίαι, that this Thalia-rich, famous tribute connects the flowering of the city in the form of festivals and fame with the flourishing of its men. This contributes to the assumed subtext of the ode, the aim to restore the young Diagoras to favor.

[34] Once again I have elected not to take χάριν as a quasi-preposition. In the phrase συμποσίου τε χάριν καδός τε τιμάσαις νέον, v.5, I take χάριν as object of τιμάσαις, along with κᾶδος, the two objects linked by τε . . . τε: "honoring the *charis* of the symposium and the new son-in-law." Further justification for this interpretation can be found in Brown 1984a, 43–44n.28.

I cultivate the choice garden of the Charites,
for those goddesses dispense the delightful things;
and men become noble and skilled because of
divine influence.

Pindar Ol. 9.27–29

The passage is reminiscent of Pindar's cult-hymn to the
Charites, the *Fourteenth Olympian Ode*, in which he addresses the Charites as dispensers of things "sweet and
delightful" to mortals, to individuals who are "skilled,
beautiful, glorious" (5–7). In both passages it is clear that
receiving inspiration from the Charites, getting one's poetic
skills from them, becoming *sophos*,[35] was on a par with other
privileged positions in Pindar's world—moving in the circuit of the nobles, being beautiful, attractive to others, or
being one of the glorious victors.

Bacchylides speaks of the poet's good fortune in receiving
honor from the Charites, a gift that raised one's expectations
as it raised one's station in life: One was acknowleged as a
poet or a prophet:

ἢ γὰρ σ[ο]φὸς ἢ Χαρίτων τιμὰν λελογχώς
ἐλπίδι χρυσέᾳ τέθαλεν
ἢ τινα θευπροπίαν
    εἰδώς·

For when one is inspired, either through receiving
the good fortune of honor from the Charites
or through knowing something of an oracular strain,
one flourishes with hope that is golden.

Bacchylides 10.39–42

But this gift of inspiration, akin to having oracular powers, is
ephemeral. It comes unexpectedly, as if by lot. The Charites
bestow favor on those whom they choose, and mortals can
but acknowledge their good fortune and hope for more.
Such blessing is as precious as it is precarious. Being singled

---

[35] For the connection between σοφός and skill in poetry, see Woodbury
1985, 200–201.

out for a stroke of the good fortune represented by the Charites does not go unnoticed by others. In his first ode, Bacchylides describes the reaction of those who see a lucky
recipient of the Charites' favor: They stare at him in amaze-
ment (151–52).

A poet who can cultivate the choice garden of the Charites, culling the choice flowers therein (*Isth.* 8.17), is able to
make his work alluring, attractive, fecund. In the *Sixth Pythian* Ode, Pindar is the gardener, "turning over again the
garden of Aphrodite or the Charites"'(1–2).[36] The inclusion
of the love-goddess may be personal, because of a special
relationship between the poet and the victor's son,[37] but it is
also likely to be conventional, describing the potential of his
work to exercise irresistible charm, like the allurement of a
beloved. In the game of *eros*, the persuasive power of *charis*
acts in conjunction with Aphrodite to produce beauty that is
irresistible. But this charm is as effective in song as it is in the
human body. Like the love goddess, Charis adorns all
things, making them "winsome." When these become the
subject of song, they have a softening effect on the audience:[38]

Χάρις δ', ἅπερ ἅπαντα τεύχει τὰ μείλιχα θνατοῖς
ἐπιφέροισα τιμάν· καὶ ἄπιστον ἐμήσατο πιστόν
ἔμμεναι τὸ πολλάκις·

---

[36] On garden imagery as an example of Pindar's self-reference as a poet,
see Gianotti 1975, 71.

[37] The *Second Isthmian* Ode, also addressed to Thrasyboulus, refers to
Aphrodite and the composition of love songs; fr. 124 is a symposiastic song
sent to Thrasyboulus.

[38] Here is one of the best statements of the basic idea of χάρις, the notion
that underlies its various presentations—pleasure that provokes a response. In love the softening effect of χάρις results in an exchange of favors
between lovers. In the *First Olympian* Ode, Pelops relies upon the gifts of
Aphrodite which he exchanged with Poseidon, to lay claim to the god's
favor. This is described as τι . . . ἐς χάριν τέλλεται, "something that is
brought to fulfilment as *charis*" (76). On χάρις as the gratification in love
leading to acts of gratitude, see Gerber 1982, 119–20.

Charis, who fashions all things winsome for mortals,
adding honor and often making even the incredible
tale appear to be credible.

Pindar *Ol.* 1.30–32

The work of *charis* in poetry is to soften an audience. This
releases in them responses they might not otherwise make,
akin to being touched by love.[39] Now we can complete the
picture of the praise process. The *charis* of the song honors
the victor not by exaggeration nor, on the other hand, by
simply laying bare the facts (*alatheia*). It cloaks the facts with
the charm of beautiful verse and music, in such a way that
an audience wants to hear it and is drawn into the entire
praise event. Bacchylides appeals to the Charites at the
opening of his ninth ode to make his message succeed by
"persuading mortals" (2). This resembles Menelaus' successful plea for the restitution of Helen. Communing with
the Charites, he is able to stir up the Greeks to join the
expedition to Troy, because they give him a voice that has
magical charm:

Πλεισθενίδας Μενέλαος γάρυϊ θελξιεπεῖ
φθέγξατ', εὐπέπλοισι κοινώσας Χάρισσιν·

Menelaus son of Pleisthenes, communing with the
fair-robed Charites,
spoke with a voice of enchantment.

Bacchylides 15.48–49

Words like "fair-robed," "deep-girdled," or "violet-eyed"
are imported from the erotic to the poetic context to indicate
that the Charites' beauty gives poets the ability to charm
with speech.

The effect of such winsome praise is to make the celebrated mortal "blessed" (e.g., *Isth.* 5.12, *Nem.* 1.10–12, *Ol.*
11.1–6). This is a state akin to possessing the bliss of the
gods and as such is precarious. At the end of Pindar's *Seventh Olympian* Ode, Pindar reminds his audience of the

---

[39] Χάρις, by exerting her power on Pindar's song, will make his revision
of the myth of Pelops credible.

short-lived experience of such blessedness. He describes the joy of a *charis*-celebration but follows this with a sobering reflection. The victor's famous clan enjoys their festivities while the whole city joins in (93–94), but their joy is subject to the momentary change of the winds, which blow now in one direction, now in another (95). High achievements, with songs to commemorate them, exalt the celebrand to a state of near-divinity, but this privilege can never be more than temporary. The sentiment expressed in Solon's famous dictum "Let no man call himself blessed before his death" (Hdt. 1.32) is the subject of Bacchylides' fifth ode: Blessed is he to whom the gods apportion beauty, wealth, etc. but no one who walks on earth can be said to be happy in all respects (50–55).

The frailty of happiness and good fortune only underscores the depth and totality of the pleasure felt when one moves from darkness into the light of divine blessing. The best-known Pindaric passage describing this experience is found in the *Eighth Pythian* Ode. Mortals are subject to the uncertain fortunes that befall them with each day, and their substance is short-lived. Indeed, they are but dreamlike shadows until they receive the god-granted gleam, a divine shaft of light that makes them visible to all and makes life gentle (*Pyth.* 8.92–97). Pindar, as praise-poet, was an instrument of the divine Charites in making the life of mortals "gentle" (cf. the poet's "gentle *charites*" of *Isth.* 3.7). He rescues them from their shadowy existence and the harsh vicissitudes of fate.

"Never let the pure light of the singing Charites leave me," Pindar says (*Pyth.* 9.89–90). This light is dazzling; it illuminates the victor with a flash of fire:

᾽Αλεξιβιάδα, σὲ δ᾽ ἠύκομοι φλέγοντι Χάριτες.

Alexibiades, the fair-tressed Charites set you on fire.

Pindar *Pyth.* 5.45

The verb *phlegô*, when used transitively, is a strong word, with overtones more intense than that of simple illumination. Even when used metaphorically, it retains a close association with fire, predicated of torches, Zeus' thunderbolt, etc. Alexibiades in *Pyth*. 5 is not simply radiant in the light of the attention of the Charites, he is set ablaze.[40] In a remarkable passage, Pindar describes himself as lighting up the Locrian city of Opus with "fierce, fiery songs":

ἐγὼ δέ τοι φίλαν πόλιν
μαλεραῖς ἐπιφλέγων ἀοιδαῖς

I will set afire your own dear city
with the devouring blaze of song

Pindar *Ol*. 9.21–22

The "devouring" aspect of the word *maleros* ("greedy") is hard to reconcile with the glorifying process of praise songs. But a burning, devouring passion was characteristic of *charis*-cognates (e.g., *charopos*, "bright-eyed") when they described hot desire, and this explains the fiery work of the Charites and their praise poet. A victor and his city, when celebrated in song, are made passionately happy. They greet the praise as a *charopos* lion his prey (*Il*. 3.23), and their desire for it is fittingly described as fiery or blazing. Praise-songs kindled desire into a flame that hungrily devoured praise as the songs were sung.

The source of this glorifying light was, of course, the gods. Pindar gives eloquent expression to the collective longing for this divine light in the opening of the *Fifth Isthmian* Ode. He praises Theia, mother of the sun god Helios, for on her account people prize gold above all else and strive for glory in such mortal pursuits as seafaring and the athletic games (1–11). Theia, mother of the sun (and of the moon and dawn, Hes. *Theog*. 371) was a light-divinity, and hence was "mother of the eyes" (Pindar, *Pae*. 9.2). Theia's regency over glory can be explained by her presiding over the "on-looking" of mortals and gods at the moment when a person was made "visible in glory."[41]

---

[40] The image is no doubt real as well as metaphorical. The song-celebrations could last into the evening and take place in torchlight. (*Ol*. 10.73–75).

[41] Fränkel 1975, 486, identifies Theia with "the power which in every

This divine power was represented among the Charites by Aglaia, the light-glorifying one. Bacchylides says of Hieron's great victory in the chariot race at Olympia in 468 B.C.E. that it was won "with Aglaia" (3.6). The victory celebration is an *"aglaia-kômos"* (*Ol.* 3.6). But gifts from the gods are part of a reciprocal transaction, and the work of Aglaia in assuring Hieron's glory was not unrelated to his glorifying Delphi with brightly visible golden tripods, as Croesus had done. Bacchylides makes sure that the connection is not missed: "Let men bring the god *aglaia*-glory," he insists, "the best assurance of happiness" (21–22). This advice is reinforced by the mythical account of Croesus. The Lydian king's generosity with glory-gifts to the god of Delphi was the basis of his agonized cry from the funeral pyre:

πο]ῦ θεῶν ἐστιν χάρις;

Where is the *charis* of the gods?

Bacchylides 3.38

His prayer for reciprocal help is answered. Zeus sends a rain cloud to quench the fire, and Apollo carries him with his daughters to the land of the Hyperboreans, utopian people who escape the usual constraints of mortality (*Pyth.* 10.42–44). The parallel gifts of Croesus and Hieron, with the god's response, provide the structure for the entire ode, with Apollo, light-glorification, and the *charis* of return favors permeating the whole. Croesus' outlay earns him an escape from death, while Hieron's earns him immortality in song. The *charis* belonging to each occurs at strategic moments in both accounts (38, 97), and the verbal echo at these two points may be deliberate.

This requital of favors obeyed the unwritten rule of *dikê*, "justice through equilibrium," and was contrasted in Greek

---

field creates and establishes value as something valued and binding." This is possible because she is progenitor of illumination, hence vision, making it possible that "all admirable works on earth are visible." Further on Theia, see Wilamowitz 1922, 200–205; Fränkel 1927, 63; Gundert 1935, 11–13; Dornseiff 1933, 79; Treu 1965, 90; and Bremer 1976, 255–58.

thought with "excessive, one-sided behavior," *hybris*.[42]
Charis, which adhered to the rules of *dikê*, brought people
together; *hybris* divided them. Apollo carried the lyre,
which was a "possession operating according to *dikê*" (*Pyth.*
1.2). He also carried a bow, with which he defeated the
giants and their *hybris* (*Pyth.* 8.11–12, 17–18).[43] This ode
opens with an invocation to Hesychia (Tranquility), who is
"daughter of Dika (Justice)." The poet asks her to receive
the victor's celebration as one kindly disposed, knowing
that she, like Apollo, can be harsh when confronted with
hybris (8–12). The victor has already earned a kindly reception from Apollo (18). This, the favorable disposition of the
gods, is to be cultivated, says Pindar, for it brings the greatest gains (13–14). The victor's city, Aegina, had a history of
justice and moderation which had earned for it just such a
blessing. This is described as a lucky throw of the dice:
Aegina "fell not far from the Charites" (21). The result was
that the city became conspicuous for the heroes and athletic
victors reared there, and its reputation reached a final perfection when these heroes and men were celebrated in song
(24–27). Such a song is described by Pindar as "gentle" celebration (31), like the praise hymn that "raises up the victor
with the gentle *charites*" (*Isth.* 3.8). The Charites and *charis*
are at home in a gentle social context, with *dikê*, harmony,
balance—in a word, with civility. Aegina's lot in "falling
near the Charites" was a reward for observing the laws of
civilized behavior. The victory party, a symposium, also o-
beyed these laws. "Peace loves the symposium," says Pin-

---

[42] For general discussions of the concept of justice in early Greek
thought, and its tight connection with the notion of equilibrium, see Lloyd-
Jones 1983; Havelock 1978; and Vlastos 1947, 156–78.

[43] For Apollo's performance on the lyre, which alternated with that of
the Muses, producing a "concordant" balance of performers, and which
obeyed the rules of *dikê*, see Bernardini 1979, 79–85. The lyre provided for
harmoniai by the tension between its high and low notes. Just so the bow, of
comparable shape, was under tension (παλίντονος, "bent back upon itself," Heraclitus, 12 B 51 DK, cf. *Od.* 21.11 and *Il.* 10.459) and was used to
execute *dikê* in the social sphere by punishing wrongdoing.

dar, and it is at the symposium that the gentle victory-ode is
sung, making the victory blossom (*Nem.* 9.48–49).[44]

At the heart of the gentle civility that enjoyed tranquility
and the blessing of the gods was, of course, a respect for
others. More specifically, it entailed a respect for the *moirai*
of others, their share of privileges which had been apportioned by the gods. Appropriating an excessive share for
oneself constituted *hybris*, setting up an imbalance and in-
viting reprisal. Refusal to award a due portion of honor to
another was a form of *hybris*, like ignoring the code of reciprocity. The figure of Ixion in Pindar's *Second Pythian* Ode
constitutes such a violation of civility, and Pindar gives us an
account in which a full understanding of *charis* and the
Charites is crucial.

The ode is written to celebrate a chariot victory for Hieron, and it opens with praise of his gentle restraining
powers over his horses. His hands, like those of the *charites*
in the *Third Isthmian* Ode (8), are "gentle," and the wheels of
the chariot are compliant—they "obey the bit" (*Pyth* 2.11).
The harnessing of the horses and car sets the scene as one of
tempered strength.[45] Taming, the restraining of brute in-
stincts, constitutes the essence of civilized behavior. Pindar
makes the claim that among the best demonstrations of civility are fine-sounding praise-songs that will compensate
the victor for excellent performance (14). He follows this
claim with examples of other public proclamations of praise,
directed at kings and other benefactors as acts of gratitude.
The legendary priest-king of Cyprus, Cinyras, had brought
good fortune to his people with divine help (*Nem.* 8.17–18).
In the *Second Pythian* Ode, we are told that Cinyras' subjects
are moved by *charis* to reciprocate:

ἄγει δὲ χάρις
φίλων ποί τινος ἀντὶ ἔργων ὀπιζομένα·

[44] For a discussion of the importance of calm tranquility to the symposium, see Slater 1981, 205–14.

[45] For the effect of cumulative vocabulary like ἀγαναῖσιν and πεισι-
χάλινα, see Lefkowitz 1976, 16.

charis, filled with awe,
takes the lead, surely, responding to someone's kindly deeds.

Pindar *Pyth.* 2.17

The praise of the Cyprians for their kind king, often repeated (15), ensured the continuation of his name and fame down through the generations.[46] But the important words here are "*charis* takes the lead." It is *charis* that prompts one to respond, for the pleasure of being treated kindly moves one to act. *Charis* in this context is described as *opizomena*, filled with that feeling of wonder and awe that accompanies the coming face-to-face (the *ops* of *opizomena*) with majesty, with people or actions of an extraordinary character. The tone of this ode, in which Pindar focuses on his responsibility to praise Hieron's greatness, suggests that the response of praise derives from a feeling of indebtedness and subservience.[47] This may be so when kings receive gratitude from their subjects, but subservience is not inherent in *charis*: A *charis*-response issues from a deeply felt pleasure of a social nature, and its source need not be someone of superior rank. Hieron, like Cinyras, has already had a share of public praise, from a woman of Epizephyrian Locri. His intervention in the anticipated attack on Locri by Anaxilas, a tyrant from Messena and Rhegium, had ensured the safety of the Locrians.[48] The grateful woman calls out her praise from her doorway, now that she is able to look out with security (20).

[46] The use of the present tense κελαδέοντι (15) suggests that the Cyprians are still spreading the word of Cinyras' benefits in Pindar's day. The good reputation of Cinyras, reported in Homer (*Il.* 11.20), was still alive in Roman times (see Farnell 1932, 12 *ad* 15–18).

[47] Most 1985, 76, says of this passage: "The multitude of parallels serves to liberate χάρις from a too restrictive definition of felt gratitude to a benefactor in response to specific benefits, and generalizes the term to include an attitude of reverence towards those who are ontologically superior to oneself."

[48] For the sources that refer to this historical event, see Woodbury 1978, 287–91.

These vignettes are followed by the mythical account of Ixion, a negative exemplar of the obligation to praise and to behave with civility. Unlike the Cyprians, Ixion could not bear the responsibility that came with a great amount of good fortune. His privilege had been to enjoy consort with the gods, but his *hybris* was as great as his honor had been. Lusting after Hera, he ignored the boundary established between mortals and immortals. He crossed the limits of his *moira*, the measured apportionment appropriate for his station (34). Further, he didn't reciprocate the kindness of his hosts, who had offered him a sweet life among the gods (25–26). His punishment in the first instance was to find emptiness instead of fulfilment: The woman to whom he made love was "empty," a cloud, and the sweetness he pursued was an illusion (37). Further, he and his offspring are isolated from human society, from the Charites:

ἄνευ οἱ Χαρίτων τέκεν γόνον ὑπερφίαλον
μόνα καὶ μόνον οὔτ' ἐν ἀν-
δράσι γερασφόρον οὔτ' ἐν θεῶν νόμοις·

Without the Charites she bore him a monstrous race;
she alone, a lonely race, and unworthy of honor
among men or from the dispensations of the gods.

Pindar *Pyth.* 2.42–43

The departure of *charis* or the Charites is associated with a fracture inside society, human or divine, and the repetition *mona kai monon* (43) insists upon their condition as isolated specimens.[49] The offspring will not receive a birth gift of honor (48) as would a normal divine child, nor as human could he join others in sacrifice to the gods; he is *hyperphialon* (lit., "beyond libation"). Ixion had broken the rules that governed a healthy society, and he and his offspring were punished accordingly—with exile, loss of society.

Ixion's final punishment was to be yoked to the *iunx*, the

---

[49] For a good discussion of the isolation of Ixion and his progeny, see Bell 1984, 12.

ever-turning wheel used in love charms. As he whirled around, he repeated a "message that was of import to everyone" (41):

τὸν εὐεργέταν ἀγαναῖς
ἀμοιβαῖς ἐποιχομένους τίνεσθαι

One must repay the benefactor
with gentle returns, over and over again.

Pindar *Pyth.* 2.24

Like the wheel of punishment that is ever turning, the cyclical, reciprocal acts of kindness are freshly renewed as people respond with gentleness to one another. They have tamed strength that might otherwise injure, like the taming hands of Hieron. Favors need to be "discharged" (*tinesthai*), like debts; actions of requital are called for and the cycle, like Ixion's wheel, never stops: Fresh favors are proffered and reciprocated.

The obligation to requite favors is nowhere more forcefully stated in Greek poetry. In the *Second Pythian* Ode, Pindar is voicing the specific obligation to render praise in return for actions undertaken by people of superior status. This is the milieu of praise poetry. As an epinician poet, Pindar gives voice to the gratitude and awe of the people who surround someone momentarily raised to a higher status, the victor. This epinician *charis* is the "*charis* that is filled with awe," (*opizomena*, 17), which Pindar sharply contrasts with calumny, characteristic of some of the poetry of Archilochus (54–56). Archilochus elected to set himself apart as independent of, and at times hostile to, his community. His poetry was self-directed, not other-directed and, in Pindar's view, he suffered the consequences. "Fattened" (56) by the abuse of others, in his isolation he, like Ixion, was ultimately without resources, helpless, says Pindar (54).

After the mention of Archilochus, the ode shifts quickly, as if to reinforce Pindar's stance within his society, which is firmly opposed to the poetry of blame, hence suitably rewarded. There follows an invitation to others to accept the *charis* of his song:

τὸ Καστόρειον δ' ἐν Αἰολίδεσσι χορδαῖς θέλων
ἄθρησον χάριν ἑπτακτύπου
φόρμιγγος ἀντόμενος.

Consider with good will the Castor song in Aeolian tuning,
going to greet it, a *charis*[50]
of the seven-stringed lyre.

Pindar *Pyth.* 2.69–71

Charis brings us back to the realm of favor and reciprocity, and civilized behavior. Mention of Rhadamanthys (73) reinforces the association of requital, the appropriateness of rewards as of punishments.[51] Ixion and Archilochus paid the price for their selfish, asocial behavior. Pindar, on the other hand, hopes to reap the payment for his work as a poet of praise, and the reward is social:

ἁδόν-
τα δ' εἴη με τοῖς ἀγαθοῖς ὁμιλεῖν.

May it be my place to give pleasure to the noble
and to keep their company.

Pyth. 2.96

⁵⁰ χάρις is once again taken here as an appositive. It is important at this juncture that χάρις bear its full weight, recalling the analogous χάρις of the Cyprians (17). For the foreshadowing of this by the χαῖρε of 67, see Lefkowitz 1976, 25.

⁵¹ ῥέζοντά τι καὶ παθεῖν ἔοικεν: "the doing and the suffering should be of one kind" (*Nem.* 4.32), a principle ascribed to Rhadamanthys in Aristotle's *Nicomachean Ethics* 5.1132b25. Further, see Most (above, n. 47) 106–7.

Chapter Seven

THE *CHARIS* OF THE *ORESTEIA*

IN THE *ORESTEIA* of Aeschylus, we get a first glimpse
of the secularization of *charis*. Under pressure from the
rising city-state, patterns of human behavior altered.
Whereas formerly the individual's choice of action was dictated by the collective will of a small group—the clan and
townspeople of Pindar's victors, the comrades of Achilles
and Agamemnon—and was measured against the universally accepted will of the gods, now there was room to ex-
periment with new possibilities. Allegiances became detached from the intensely personal and were based on more
diffuse, civic loyalties. *Charis*, which had held two individuals in a tightly bound nexus of reciprocal favoring, was on
the way to standing for the political favors that bought one's
way in the Hellenistic city. Like the other cardinal virtues of
the archaic Greek world which had been accepted as universal, absolute, divinely endorsed, *charis* now came under the
secular banner of "man is the measure." One person's *charis*
competed with the *charis*-claim of another; the two might
even be mutually exclusive, the triumph (pleasure) of one
entailing the defeat (pain) of the other.

Such social transformations never occur quickly. From a
distance we can observe the provisional attempts at new
possibilities of behavior, where congruencies and contradictions between the old and the new are absorbed here and
there, until there emerges a consistent pattern that fits com-
fortably within the new order. In the tragedies of the mid
and late fifth century we encounter the intense, pained self-
questioning that accompanied this social transformation.
When personal claims came into conflict with one another,
where was the ultimate court of appeal? If the very under-
pinnings of justice, of *dikê*, were made relative to the needs

of the respective claimants, where or from whom could one seek final arbitration? Poets best transmit the wounds and agonies of society in dislocation, and, beginning with the poetry of Aeschylus, we get a plea for resolution which, in its painful grappling with contradictions, exposes the competing values in their barest form.

In the *Oresteia*, the protagonists demonstrate the harsh reality that justice is achieved by violence. If *charis* is linked with justice, referring to the pleasure that comes with the imposition of order, then *charis* too, that gentle, deeply felt personal joy that comes with the conferring of a gift, or kindness, will also result from violence:

στάζει δ' ἔν γ' ὕπνῳ πρὸ καρδίας
μνησιπήμων πόνος. καὶ παρ' ἄ -
κοντας ἦλθε σωφρονεῖν.
δαιμόνων δέ που χάρις βίαιος[1]
σέλμα σεμνὸν ἡμένων.

Woe-remembering agony drips before my heart
as I sleep. Learning to act prudently
comes even to those who are reluctant.
But in some wise there is a *charis* that comes with violence,
a *charis* of the gods enthroned on their awful seat.

Ag. 179–83

The chorus of elders in Argos are awaiting the outcome of the war in Troy in which they were too frail to fight. From a distance they can reflect upon the chain of violence and pain that began with the rape of Helen. They take refuge in the thought that the gods, maintaining order in the cosmos, impose coercion in order to teach mortals a lesson. Such coercion, pain that can never be erased from memory (180),

---

[1] The text cited here is taken from the Oxford edition of Page, 1972. The mss. have transmitted βιαίως, emended by Turnebus to βίαιος. Fraenkel 1950 and West 1990 have restored βιαίως. Whether the violence is associated directly with χάρις (as in the text adopted by Page), or with the gods who issue it, does not make a great deal of difference to the understanding of χάρις in this passage.

is at the same time pleasure (*charis*), inasmuch as it comes as a gift of the gods. Acceptance of the idea that the gods command awe (183) is old, but calling this a violent *charis* is new. The chorus accept the sacrifice of Iphigeneia as just such a violent form of instruction by the gods. Their anguish over Agamemnon's killing of his innocent daughter is mitigated by the thought that behind it lies the hand of Zeus:

τὸν φρονεῖν βροτοὺς ὁδώ-
σαντα, τὸν πάθει μάθος
θέντα κυρίως ἔχειν·

(Zeus) who has set mortals on the path
to wisdom, who has laid down as a valid decree
that learning takes place through suffering

Ag. 176–77

Just how this learning-through-suffering takes place is not clear. Iphigeneia is one who suffers, but she dies; what then is learned, by whom, and how? If the learning is done by the survivors, what type of learning is it? The degree to which intelligent reasoning is involved in the process has been the subject of considerable discussion.[2] The history of the

---

[2] Pope 1974, 100–113, argues that the φρονεῖν of 176, as elsewhere in Aeschylus, does not entail rational activity but refers simply to "consciousness" of the kind that separates men from animals, the dead, etc. (108). He describes the lesson learned as a conscious awareness that violence is simply the way the cosmos works. By violence the gods teach mortals "to heel" (σωφρονεῖν, 181).

Conacher 1976, 328–37, argues that the law of Zeus appeals to men's reasoning (331). He points to passages in Aeschylus where φρονεῖν can carry "a clear suggestion of a specific use of the mind, often to some particular moral purpose" (333). Conacher sees a dawning awareness in the chorus that the learning of this ordinance of Zeus has a moral end, that the chorus are becoming wise in however rudimentary a way, and that this foreshadows the conversion of the Erinyes at the end of the trilogy. This reading preserves the force of χάρις in 182: The lesson of Zeus is a blessing for human society. Once people see the moral purpose of this lesson—the restraining of unjust behavior for the social good—they will accept the curbs on their activity by the gods, however violent, and adapt their behavior in accordance with this wisdom they have attained.

Lloyd-Jones 1983, 85–88, is not prepared to grant this much sophistica-

House of Atreus was a chronicle of suffering, beginning with the banquet served to Thyestes, but it is difficult to see in what way its members had learned a lesson that in any way modified their behavior. If the chorus are claiming that they are now wise, in that they see the purpose of the hand of Zeus operating with avenging *Dikê*, we would expect them to lay greater stress on having seen the blessings (sc. *charis*) of moderation, not violence. Instead, they speak of the ability to act prudently as coming whether they will it or not (180).

After their proclamation that learning takes place through suffering, they describe Agamemnon's killing of Iphigeneia as his "putting on the yoke of Necessity" (217). This is not appropriate language for describing a reasoned choice on the part of Agamemnon. He was caught between two "grievously heavy" alternatives (206–7) and elected to obey the demands of Artemis. He killed Iphigeneia with the uncertain hope that "all may turn out well" (216). It is clear that he did not make his choice out of consideration for morality (facilitating a war of punishment against the Trojans), but out of fear of disobeying. By the same token, it would be doing Agamemnon (and the chorus) an injustice to say that they were incapable of deducing from the pattern of retribution in the universe that it would be better to behave prudently. The chorus is nothing if not prudent in the play; still, they are not being called upon to be moral philosophers in this passage. They are relating the sequence of events to date, observing that these follow a pattern of retribution,

---

tion to the chorus. They are, he says, simply acknowledging the inscrutability of the god. Speaking from a relatively primitive religious stance, they call upon Zeus as the supreme god of the universe, "champion of *Dikê*, the order of the universe," punishing those who challenge his ordinances. For Lloyd-Jones, χάρις βίαιος, "grace that comes by violence," consists in the punishment of men's injustices to one another (87). σωφρονεῖν (181), he translates as "thinking safely," and φρονεῖν (176) simply as "thinking." The χάρις of Zeus, then, amounts to the blessing of preserving mortals from self-destruction, and the lesson learned by the chorus is to "think safely" (and presumably behave accordingly), for the law of retribution is both inevitable and for the good of human society.

and they save themselves from despair by seeking and finding religious endorsement for this pattern. For them it would be intolerable to see the violent events as meaningless: "Somehow" (182),[3] they say, it is a gift from the gods, a *charis*. The accent is not on morality but on divinity. The ultimate source of pain and suffering brought upon Trojans and Greeks alike was the rape of Helen. As the chorus reflect upon the effects of this on the city of Troy, they call the city's destruction a *charis*: Helen in Troy was like a lion cub reared in a human family, returning a violent *charis* in exchange for its upbringing. Her recompense consisted in slaughtering the flock of her host:

χάριν
γὰρ τροφεῦσιν ἀμείβων
μηλοφόνοισι σὺν ἄταις
δαῖτ᾽ ἀκέλευστος ἔτευξεν·

returning the *charis*
to its host-parents with
flock-slaughtering woes,
it made a banquet unbidden.

Ag. 728–31

Helen owed reciprocal returns to the family that embraced her.[4] Instead, she requited with pain the pleasure she received at their hands. Aeschylus' use of *charis* in this passage is boldly ironic. Helen's performance is a fully realized form of the wraith Hera in Pindar's *Second Pythian* Ode: She is a *charis* that is in fact not a *charis*, one who requites the pleasure act with the eternal torture of her lover. Aeschylus' use of *charis* at 728 is stunning and deliberate. He reinforces his assessment of the abduction of Helen with his use of

---

[3] I take που as enclitic, not adverbial, on the analogy with the ποι of *Pyth.* 2.17, where ποι occurs in a passage in which we once again find qualified certainty being claimed about dispensations coming from the gods.

[4] One of the most commonly understood reciprocal words in Greek is the τροφεῖα, the θρέπτρα or θρεπτήρια, the nurturing of a child that called for returns to the parents when the child was grown.

kêdos at 699 to describe her relationship to Paris: The word is a convenient pun, meaning both "marriage" and "cause for grief."[5]

Troy's pain is made abundantly clear in this play, even though the play ostensibly focuses on the affairs of Troy's enemy, the Greeks, and their chief, Agamemnon. Aeschylus makes the dramatic point that pain and pleasure are correlative terms and a requital response can consist of a single action that contains both *charis* and its opposite. The pleasure that was introduced to Troy with Helen was repaid with destruction, but this was itself *charis*-pleasure for the destroyers. The erotic pleasure of Paris, his illicit enjoyment of Helen's beauty, was answered with woe. The chorus describe this as a rape of the inviolable:

> οὐκ ἔφα τις
> θεοὺς βροτῶν ἀξιοῦσθαι μέλειν
> ὅσοις ἀθίκτων χάρις
> πατοῖθ᾽· ὁ δ᾽ οὐκ εὐσεβής·

> Someone said
> that the gods do not consider it worthwhile to concern
> themselves with mortals by whom the *charis* of things
> untouchable would be trampled.
> But such a fellow is impious.

Ag. 369–72

Helen's beauty, her *charis*, is like Sappho's delicate hyacinth that was crushed under the feet of shepherds (fr. 105). But in the case of Helen, the trampling was not innocent. The abuse of Helen's beauty was an offence against the gods.[6]

---

[5] The oxymoronic word play in these two passages of Aeschylus is anticipated by Archilochus' λυγρὰ χαριζόμενοι of fr. 6 (above, Ch. 5).

[6] It is important to see the implications of the attraction of feminine beauty represented by χάρις in this passage. Fraenkel 1950, *ad loc.*, is content to extract only "thankfulness," "piety," and "delight" from the word here. Denniston and Page 1957, *ad loc.*, go further in saying that "there is *grace*, almost *charm* or *beauty*, in the sanctities on which the sinner tramples." But there is more here than "almost-beauty": there is the renowned beauty of Helen which was violated, an act that will not go unpunished by Zeus Xenios, as the chorus pronounce (362–69).

Paris, in taking Helen, violates the laws of hospitality enforced by Zeus Xenios, and the god retaliates with a killing stroke (367), a *charis* that comes with violence. Behind this lies a thought that is more unsettling. Agamemnon, like Troy, will receive a mortal blow, and the blow will come from his wife. Helen caused the eventual destruction of Troy and Agamemnon will die as a result of crushing the beauty of his innocent daughter. If these are instances of a violent *charis* that comes from the gods, does this mean that Clytemnestra, who will administer the blow to her husband, is an instrument of the gods' punishment? This is certainly her claim (1525).

Zeus, in punishing Troy, redresses the balance required by Justice. By this same pain-inflicting act, he confers the pleasure of honor on the victorious Greeks:

χάρις γὰρ οὐκ ἄτιμος εἴργασται πόνων.

A *charis* of woes that is not without honor has been accomplished.

Ag. 354

It is this brutal pattern of just violence in which the chorus of elders place their trust. But a gift from the gods, as *charis*, commands an expression of gratitude. The Greek herald, arriving in Argos and confirming the rumor that the Greeks had been successful at Troy, insists that there will be recompense for this *charis* of Zeus:

καὶ χάρις τιμήσεται
Διὸς τάδ᾽ ἐκπράξασα.

And the *charis* of Zeus, having
executed these things, will be honored.

Ag. 581–82

"These things," the destruction of Troy, were exacted as payment for the robbery of Helen; this was the price[7] that

---

[7] It is tempting to read into τιμήσεται the price/calculation content of τιμή, although the extent to which this was on Aeschylus' mind is, of course, impossible to gauge.

had to be paid. Menelaus and the Greeks were shamed and angered by this abduction, as Achilles was shamed by the abduction of Briseis. Such an offence called for satisfaction, the kind of gratification that came only when full payment was made, when the abductor was brought to his knees— the same psychological/moral crisis that lay at the heart of the *Iliad*. But victory over the Trojans indicated that a *charis*-relationship had been initiated by Zeus, and it called for a response. As the injury could not be forgotten until vengeance was complete, so the avenging *charis* will not be forgotten until payment is made in full to the gods. This the triumphant Agamemnon promises upon his return:

τούτων θεοῖσι χρὴ πολύμνηστον χάριν
τίνειν, ἐπείπερ χἀρπαγὰς ὑπερκόπους
ἐπραξάμεσθα

We must pay back to the gods a *charis*
that is much-remembering of these things,
because we have exacted payment for an outrageous rape

Ag. 821–23

Other thank offerings are proposed, this time by Clytemnestra, but unlike those promised by her husband, which are a genuine *charis*, hers are counterfeit, like the joy she feigns at seeing Agamemnon again. The chorus criticize her overzealous call for rites of thanksgiving, premature in nature, as one would expect of a woman. The people of Argos are being asked to join the queen in anticipating an act of *charis* when it is not yet at hand:

γυναικὸς αἰχμᾷ πρέπει
πρὸ τοῦ φανέντος χάριν ξυναινέσαι·

It is to be expected in the rule of a woman
that one join in the praise of *charis* before the object itself
appears.

Ag. 483–84

The gift bestowed by *charis* will never appear, for the *charis* is false: Clytemnestra's feelings of pleasure she erroneously attributes to Agamemnon's safe return. Her excitement is the result not of this, but of accomplishing a personal scheme that has little to do with gratitude. The true rites of thanksgiving never occur, but the artifice intensifies. Clytemnestra prepares for the murder of her husband and exults in the possibility that Agamemnon, along with Cassandra, can be a substitute for animal victims normally slaughtered on the altar. The king and his lover constitute her *charis* for the gods:

τὰ μὲν γὰρ ἑστίας μεσομφάλου
ἕστηκεν ἤδη μῆλα † πρὸς σφαγὰς † πυρός,
ὡς οὔποτ' ἐλπίσασι τήνδ' ἕξειν χάριν.

The animals are already standing before the central hearth ready for the sacrificial fire,
victims who never expected to have this *charis*.

Ag. 1056–58

Verses 1057–58 present serious textual difficulties, and 1058 was excised by Fraenkel (1950) following Wilamowitz, partly on the grounds that Clytemnestra would not be engaging in an emotional flourish at this point. But, as Denniston and Page (1957) point out, this is an unnecessary sidestepping of the emotion that dominates the scene. Clytemnestra's emotions are intense and operate on several levels at once. She urges Cassandra to hurry inside to join Agamemnon for the sacrifice, a cruel pretext to get the girl to sacrifice her own body beside Agamemnon's. The passage leaves us with one serious question:[8] For whom is this sacrifice an unexpected *charis*? If it belongs to the victims standing at the altar (the *mêla* of 1057), we can read it as a sinister comment of Clytemnestra's that Agamemnon and Cassandra are a pair of lovers who never expected to find them-

---

[8] A problem arises because there is no plural noun in the dative case to which the participle phrase οὔποτ' ἐλπίσασι can readily refer. This is the reason, I assume, that West 1990, following Maas, indicates that a line dropped out after 1058.

selves brought down by the sacrificial knife. This reading is supported by another passage in the play which refers to the "unexpected" nature of Agamemnon's homecoming: At 911 (in the carpet scene) Clytemnestra urges her handmaids to spread the purple tapestry for the king so that "Justice may lead him to his unexpected home." In addition to this, there is the possible foreshadowing of the present scene with the mention of a hearth at 851, where Agamemnon first arrives in Argos and prepares to make his way to the palace, "the home with the *hearth*." But the passage also recalls the precipitate *charis* thank-offering required of the citizens by Clytemnestra at 484. If we connect these two passages, then at 1056–58 Clytemnestra is including the townspeople and herself with those who are getting an unexpected *charis* from the murder. But we remind ourselves that Clytemnestra has expectations very different from those of the people of Argos. Her invitation to Cassandra amounts to a pretext that will get the Trojan princess inside to be killed.

There is yet another possibility for the identity of the figures who will enjoy the novel sacrifice, and no doubt with pleasure in the highest degree: Clytemnestra and Aegisthus. The brutality of a (covert) admission of this sort was prepared by the gruesome image of Helen, the lion whelp preparing a feast of "flock-murdering woes," a *charis* thank-offering to those who reared her (728–31). The identity of the victims, even if the text were secure, might have been left deliberately ambiguous by Aeschylus. All three groups of people qualify, and even more horror can be generated if the single *charis*-act accumulates, in various ways, pain for the victims and pleasure for the executioners.

The false sacrifice was, of course, a religious travesty. However, it was but a rehearsal for the savage ecstasy in which Clytemnestra exults as she stands beside the bodies of her two victims (1372–98). She brazenly describes in detail her killing of Agamemnon, when the first two blows only maimed him, but the third and mortal blow was a "welcome *charis* for Underworld Zeus":

καὶ πεπτωκότι
τρίτην ἐπενδίδωμι, τοῦ κατὰ χθονός
Διὸς νεκρῶν σωτῆρος εὐκταίαν χάριν.

And I added a third stroke
for him when he had fallen, a welcome
prayer-*charis* for Zeus, protector of the dead under the earth.

Ag. 1385–87

Charis, a word well-suited to the ritual context, is applied
here to the most brutal form of sacrilege. Clytemnestra's
ironic vocabulary builds in intensity until it reaches the climactic stroke, the third one. For the audience who saw Clytemnestra standing by Agamemnon's body in a pool of
blood (1309), her words would call to mind the third libation, wine poured into the ground like blood, normally a
cheerful libation to Zeus Soter (245–46). The votive offering
Clytemnestra chooses to call the body of her husband is the
culmination of three murders in the House of Atreus: the
children of Thyestes, Iphigeneia, then Agamemnon. This
horrific scene of blood is the brutal incarnation of the abor-
tive *charis*-offering of 484, the *charis* for Zeus announced by
the herald (581–82), promised by Agamemnon (821–23),
ominously hinted at by Clytemnestra (1058). Now, with the
beast fallen, she triumphantly proclaims her realization of
the *charis*.

Not only religious but also erotic overtones reverberate
from the words of Clytemnestra as she stands beside her
bloody husband, her *charis*, and the effect is electrifying.
The queen's delight is not only the pleasure of pure satisfaction, but it has an appetitive and gruesome sexual color. She
describes his body as "striking her with a darksome shadow
of gory dew" (Fraenkel's translation), and she rejoices with
charis-pleasure (1391), like grain in the sheath receiving
drops of rain from Zeus. The delight she takes in this gruesome reenactment of the sacred marriage between earth and
sky is further stimulated by the companion death of
Agamemnon's lover. Cassandra's body is an "added relish"
for Clytemnestra's banquet of passion:

κεῖται φιλήτωρ τοῦδ'· ἐμοὶ δ' ἐπήγαγεν
εὐνῆς⁹ παροψώνημα τῆς ἐμῆς χλιδῇ.

She lies there, his lover; he[10] has brought me
a tasty relish for the revelry of my bed.

Ag. 1446–47

The chorus raise the question about ritual offerings for the
dead king after his gory murder. They ask Clytemnestra
whether she dares to carry out the normal rites of burial for
Agamemnon. Carrying out death dirges for one's own mur-

⁹ Fraenkel 1950 followed Casaubon, Hermann, Wilamowitz, and others
in daggering εὐνῆς. Fraenkel argued that "the lust which wholly possesses
the soul of this daemonic woman at the great climax of her life is not sexual,
but the lust of revenge." (He refused to see the sexual overtones in 1391.)
He is loath to have Clytemnestra make public reference to her adulterous
behavior with Aegisthus, insisting that "even in her taunts . . . she remains
a queen." But just a few lines before (1435–36), Clytemnestra made reference to the "fire of her hearth" being "set alight" by Aegisthus. However,
even without a connection to her sexual arousal by Aegisthus, the overtones of sexual lust are unmistakable in the passage. The speech itself
merits close study as an example of a poetic treatment of emotional out-
pouring at such a pitch that several emotions are fused into one moment of
intense desire and triumphant satisfaction. In using the words "lust of
revenge," Fraenkel demonstrates the overlap of anger and sexual ardor
that occurs when one is at the height of passion. Greed for food becomes
indistinguishable from other extreme desires. At the peak of passion, objects of desire or sources of satisfaction can become indistinguishable. This
is reflected in the vocabulary we use for all three of these desires: We speak
not only of the "lust" for revenge but of an "appetite" for revenge, or of a
sexual "appetite."

West 1990 has restored the daggers around εὐνῆς, although seemingly
on textual grounds rather than from a sense of Victorian decorum. The
mss. have preserved the genitive χλιδῆς, which was emended by Mus-
grave to the dative χλιδῇ. This emendation has the disadvantage of sitting
awkwardly with the genitives τῆς ἐμῆς, as Denniston and Page 1957, *ad loc.*,
point out. Restoring the genitive χλιδῆς makes εὐνῆς problematic.

[10] Denniston and Page 1957, *ad loc.*, argue that the subject of ἐπήγαγεν
can be either Cassandra or Agamemnon. But it was Agamemnon who
"led" Cassandra to Clytemnestra—quite literally—in his chariot. The
emendation of Blaydes 1898 of ἀνήρ for εὐνῆς is attractive, inasmuch as it,
together with the δ' in the preceding line, would clearly articulate a change
of subject from the "she" in κεῖται.

der victim would be an oxymoronic performance, they say, using language that reflects a new mode of thinking, the sophistic embrace of paradox. Such an act would be an *acharis charis*, a *"charis* that is an un-*charis"*:

ἢ σὺ τόδ' ἔρξαι τλήσῃ, κτείνασ'
ἄνδρα τὸν αὑτῆς ἀποκωκῦσαι
ψυχῇ τ' ἄχαριν χάριν ἀντ' ἔργων
μεγάλων ἀδίκως ἐπικρᾶναι;

Do you really dare to perform these things,
to mourn over a husband whom you have killed
with your own hands, and to fulfil for his shade
an un-*charis charis* in return for his mighty deeds,
an injustice?

Ag. 1542–45

In form, such rites are a *charis*, inasmuch as they are ostensibly a response to the king's great accomplishments. But in effect they are invalid as *charis* because they are detached from *dikê* (1545). They are "unjust" in that they do not confer honor commensurate with the king's accomplishments. The calculation is wrong. In the *Choephoroi* Orestes will call them a "feeble *charis*" for the dead. They fall short of paying for the offense, which will only be paid for in full with the queen's death:

θανόντι δ' οὐ φρονοῦντι δειλαία χάρις
ἐπέμπετ'· οὐκ ἔχοιμ' ἂν εἰκάσαι τόδε·
τὰ δῶρα μείω δ' ἐστὶ τῆς ἁμαρτίας.

A feeble *charis* was sent to the unconscious dead.
I am at a loss how to assess this:
The gifts are more trivial than her offense.

Cho. 517–19

In the *Prometheus Bound* we meet another impotent *charis*. The chorus ask the hero whether his gift of fire to mortals was really a *charis*-favor:

φέρε πῶς χάρις ἁ χάρις,[11] ὦ φίλος,
εἰπέ, ποῦ τις ἀλκά;

Tell me, how is the *charis* a *charis*, my friend?
Where is there any potency in it?

Prometheus Vinctus 545–46

It was not a *charis*, explain the chorus, for it was not potent
enough to solicit an equivalent favor; mortals are too weak
to yield a return on this scale. Creatures subject to the day
can give no help to others. They are as feeble as dreams,
blind, held in bondage by the gods (546–47). Clytemnestra's
actions are brazen, to be sure, but potent they are not. Like
the puny returns Prometheus can expect from the mortals
he has protected, Clytemnestra's offerings lack the force of
equivalent kindness, of *dikê*.[12]

At the opening of the *Choephoroi*, we meet the chorus of
libation bearers dispatched to Agamemnon's tomb by Clytemnestra. They begin their great *kommos* (procession of
rhythmic lamentation) with a plea to heed the demands of
forsaken *Dikê*:

τοὐφειλόμενον
πράσσουσα Δίκη μέγ' ἀυτεῖ·

Dike cries loud,
pressing for what is due!

Cho. 310–11

When these dues are properly paid, the same pattern will be
enforced as that which emerged at Troy: One and the same
act of requital will produce both suffering and satisfaction.
The murderer will suffer, the avenger will rejoice. Orestes is
ready with a funeral gift for his father that is genuine and

[11] Triclinius gives us ἄχαρις χάρις for the unmetrical χάρις ἄχαρις of the
mss. This would be, as Griffith argues (1983 *ad loc.*), an unusual combination with φέρε; hence the text above, proposed by Sikes and Willson,
adopted by Page and by Griffith.

[12] For discussions of reciprocity in this passage, see Conacher 1980, 55–
56, and Griffith 1983, 186 and 204nn.631–34.

part of a reciprocal sequence. It will elicit from the dead king a return gift, but this will be a "gift that is a match for the evils done" (95). Somehow Orestes will receive from Agamemnon the return favor of power, the power to kill his mother.

This is what was missing in Clytemnestra's gifts, more paltry than called for by her offense, inadequate payment. The necessary parity between crime and punishment demands another round of bloody requital, but on new terms. *Dikê*, once absolute, can now be appropriated for the private desires of individuals. Like two furious incarnations of battle, *Dikê* will contend with another *Dikê* in a personal and violent *agôn* of vengeance:

Ἄρης Ἄρει ξυμβαλεῖ, Δίκᾳ Δίκα.

War god will contend with War god, *Dikê* with *Dikê*.

Cho. 461

Agamemnon, with whom resides the power of chthonic *dikê*, is pictured by Orestes as lying on the ground like a defeated wrestler. But he can still, as an underworld hero, release vengeance, which will act through his children to get the grip on his opponent, as he had been in Clytemnestra's grip (497–99). This type of vengeance is driven by anger, anger that was greatly feared in chthonic figures. But chthonic anger is quickly converted to *charis*-joy, once it is appeased, satisfied. The chorus contemplates Orestes, filled with the strength to execute the necessary deed. He will possess the strength of Perseus awash with the blood of the Gorgon, bringing *charis*:

Περσέως δ' ἐν φρεσὶν
καρδίαν < > σχεθὼν
τοῖς θ' ὑπὸ χθονὸς φίλοις
τοῖς τ' ἄνωθεν πρόπρασσ' ὧν χάρις,
Γοργοῦς λυγρᾶς <τοῖς> ἔνδοθεν
φόνιον ἄταν τιθείς[13]

---

[13] West 1990 inserts τλᾶθι in the lacuna and takes χάριν (an emendation

Having the heart of Perseus
in your breast
do for your friends, those beneath the earth
and those above, (things) in which there is *charis*,
bringing the bloody ruin of the dread Gorgon
inside the house.

Cho. 831–36

Bloody ruin becomes a *charis*. This conversion is represented graphically in the version of the Orestes legend in which chthonic female figures change from black to white when the young hero-murderer makes the appropriate ritual sacrifice (Paus. 8.34.1–3, Ch. 3 above). Similarly, at the tomb of Agamemnon, it is only when the dead king has been satisfied by appropriate ritual that he will release his power, his *charis*. The libation bearers, carrying inappropriate gifts from Clytemnestra, describe their duties in terms

---

of Emperius) as object of προπράσσων, which occurs in M (with χαρίτος). The text becomes

Περσέως τ᾽ ἐν φρεσίν
<τλᾶθι> καρδίαν σχεθών
τοῖς θ᾽ ὑπὸ χθονὸς φίλοις
τοῖς τ᾽ ἄνωθεν προπράσσων χάριν,
Γοργοῦς λυγρᾶς ἔνδοθεν
φόνιον ἄταν τιθείς

Having the heart of Perseus in your breast
be bold, exacting *charis* for your friends,
both those beneath the earth and those above,
having brought the bloody ruin of the dread Gorgon
inside the house.

Cho. 831–36

This is an attractive reading, one that preserves the familiar notion of exacting χάρις. For a full discussion of the various emendations that have been applied to this problematic text, see Garvie 1986 *ad loc.* The sense of the passage is clear, despite the variety of possible readings. Orestes is to be emboldened like the hero Perseus, inflicting destruction upon the household. If Γοργοῦς is kept in 835 (an emendation of Kirchoff, M has ὀργᾶς), then Orestes = Perseus has access to the power of the decapitated Medusa to avenge the murder of his father.

similar to those used by the chorus of elders in the *Agamemnon*: The duties are an *acharis charis*. In the first play, the gifts were disqualified as *charis* because they did not repay favors to Agamemnon. In the *Choephoroi*, they are invalid because they, like the fire of Prometheus, are powerless to elicit return-*charis*. Proper obsequies for the dead performed an apotropaic function, warding off evil, acting as a benefit for the living. When the rites were ignored, or improper, they could not deter the dead from venting wrath on the living;[14] the *charis* becomes a non-*charis*. The chorus of libation bearers tremble as they pour libations on the ground, having been dispatched by a Clytemnestra who exhibited counterfeit grief. The woman is "godless," and the chorus is afraid to utter the ritual words on her behalf. A sacrilege is not apotropaic:

> τοιάνδε χάριν ἀχάριτον ἀπότροπον κακῶν,
> ἰὼ γαῖα μαῖα, μωμένα μ' ἰάλλει
> δύσθεος γυνά· φοβοῦ-
> μαι δ' ἔπος τόδ' ἐκβαλεῖν·

Such an *uncharis charis*, an averter of evils,
she is trying for in sending me,
O Mother Earth,
the godless woman; I am afraid
to utter this word.

Cho. 44–46

Unlike the invalid obsequies being offered by the libation bearers, Orestes' gift presented at the tomb of his father is a genuine *charis*, as his sister recognizes:

> ἔπεμψε χαίτην κουρίμην χάριν πατρός.

He sent a shorn lock, a *charis* for his father.

Cho. 180

In the *kommos* Orestes begins by addressing his father with a question: How can he bring light to the shade of this man,

---

[14] On this apotropaic function of funeral offerings, see Burkert 1985, 195. On the "unquiet dead," see Garland 1985, 3–6, 93–95.

enveloped in darkness, enshrouded by the obscurity of death but also by the black cloud of humiliation? Orestes knows that he must correct the imbalance wrought by this shame, with a gift that will bring the light of honor to the dead king:

σκότῳ φάος ἀντιμοι-
ρον, χάριτες δ᾽ ὁμοίως
κέκληνται γόος εὐκλεὴς
† προσθοδόμοις † ᾽Ατρείδαις.¹⁵

A light that will be a match for the darkness,
for men call them *charites* nonetheless
when there is lamentation that brings glory
for such sons of Atreus, lying before the house.

Cho. 319–22

With his gift, Orestes brought honor to the House of Atreus. This is the key; now the offering has the power to release *dikê* and earn the name of *charis*.

The final play in the trilogy, the *Eumenides*, presents the *agôn* between two models of *dikê* contending for a rightful place as the absolute form of Justice. It is Aeschylus' reflection on a subject that was hotly debated by his contemporaries and his successors: Did one impose correction upon aggressive behavior by force or by persuasion?¹⁶ The latter

---

¹⁵ On the difficulty of this line and its meaning, see Garvie 1986, *ad loc.*, who takes the hapax προσθοδόμοις to refer to the position of the tomb, and ᾽Ατρείδαις to refer to Agamemnon, not to Orestes and Electra. This is the interpretation followed here. The point is that the light of glory will be directed through the tomb to the dead king.

¹⁶ The antithesis between πειθώ and βία was much discussed by Greek thinkers who followed Aeschylus (see Buxton 1982, 58–63). The two opposing categories are found at the heart of the confrontation between the old and the new δίκη in the *Eumenides*. The new δίκη, which responds to πειθώ, is a development of δίκη which meant "what is shown" (< δείκνυμι) about the θέμιστες of the gods, but now the responsibility for determining what this is lies with the powers of human reasoning. The role of πειθώ will be to argue all sides of a case persuasively before the court, in order that the rational faculty may be stimulated to make a balanced assessment (δίκη) of the case. Hence, δίκη is the word used to refer to such cases

model of course places new faith in the faculty of human reasoning, a faith that was but dimly present in the chorus of elders in the *Agamemnon*. Loosening the concept of justice from its old nexus of vengeance was a dramatic gesture. Its trust in the human potential to grapple with destiny was a move toward the secularization argued by the sophists. But Aeschylus does not go so far: The new model of *dikê* has divine endorsement. It is also a universal, not a relative, *dikê*: It cannot be preempted by a private set of assumptions. Behind the new, as the old, *dikê* lay the belief that it represented what was shown of the will of the gods. Divine approval was still needed to determine what was right. The intellectual ferment of the mid-fifth century finds a concept like justice caught in ambivalence: *Dikê* commonly referred to both corrective vengeance and to a case in dispute which was brought before a tribunal. In the *Eumenides*, these two *dikai* walk on stage.

The ministers of the old *dikê* are the Erinyes, avenging Furies, who are pitted against divine advocates of the new *dikê*, Apollo and Athena. In the bursts of outrage from the old chthonic deities who feel their powers under threat, we get impassioned statements of the *dikê* of requital, of "getting even," of "satisfaction."

For the Erinyes, imposing *dikê* was their *moira*, the sphere of influence apportioned to them in primordial time. This, their *moira* was an honor, a *timê*, and an affront to this honor fills them with rage. Poseidon is angered on the same grounds in the *Iliad*: In the tripartite division of the world among the sons of Kronos, Zeus had taken the largest share. He had exceeded his *moira*, forgetting that Poseidon was due an equivalent share of *timê* (15.186). The *moira* of the Erinyes included the pursuit and punishment of those

---

themselves (found in the *Eumenides* with this meaning at 467 and 581). Δίχη as "revenge" and δίχη as "what is right" coexisted happily in Greek thought. In the proem of Parmenides (18 B 1 DK), the poet passes through the gates whose keys are kept by "much-avenging" *Dikê* (Δίχη πολύ-ποινος), but the poet is then launched on a journey whose "rightness" is assured by *Dikê*. See Woodbury 1966, 610.

like Orestes who had shed kindred blood. They in fact determined the confines of *dikê*. New gods, Olympians like Athena and Apollo, were acting outside these confines (162–63). We meet the Erinyes in the play as they demand from Orestes the same payment he had asked of Clytemnestra—to pay in full, with his blood, the price of the murder he had committed (268). Orestes appeals to Athena, on the grounds that killing his mother was justified requital for her murder of his father. He asks her to determine whether Clytemnestra's death was an action that complied with *dikê* (468).

The wrath of the Erinyes presents a formidable challenge for Athena. The fury they vent arises both from their function as forces of vengeance and from their feeling that they are being dishonored, but one quickly gets the sense that the more powerful question in the play is the reckoning with dishonor. They vow to discharge venom and blight the land of Athens, the ground where their rights are being undermined. They will destroy leaf and child in the name of *dikê*, casting poison upon the ground to ruin the mortals who have offended them. Once again, the calculation is exact, measure for measure: The poison will be commensurate with their grief (782).

Athena realizes that she must accommodate both grievances of the Erinyes. Their contention that cases of kin-murder must be avenged and their claim that they had been dishonored must both be satisfied. Athena admits that kin-murders and the cases that try them threaten to arouse quick and dangerous anger[17] in the loser (472). Indeed, it is beyond the capacity of any single mortal or even god to pronounce on such cases, and hence it warrants the establishment of a court of justice which will transcend any individual, partisan view of the case. But this is new, alien language for the Erinyes, and they are only appeased when

---

[17] Page 1972 takes ὀξυμηνίτου to modify φόνου; West 1990 takes it with δίκας (hence he prints ὀξυμηνίτους). In either case, the point is that the nature of the anger that surrounds the trial is dangerous.

Athena addresses their personal grievance, their sense that they have been dishonored. She promises that under the new order they will retain power and honor; indeed, they will be indispensable to every Athenian household (895–97). The effect is instantaneous. Once their rights are guaranteed by a pledge from Athena, the anger of the Erinyes vanishes. It is instantly and dramatically converted, like Orestes' white goddesses, to the disposition to confer blessings. Once again, these are commensurate with their opposite: Instead of the venom with which they were going to infect the vegetation of Athens, they promise special protection for her trees. This will be their *charis*:

δενδροπήμων δὲ μὴ πνέοι βλάβα,
τὰν ἐμὰν χάριν λέγω

May there blow no tree-blasting ruin:
this *charis* I pronounce

Eum. 938–39

They enlarge the scope of their *charis* to include the health and fertility of all crops and herds, and a blessing on marriage among the young. In cult the benefits of an agrarian society guaranteed by the Charites as vegetation goddesses evolved, with the Charites who conferred them, into the protection of civic virtues. In similar fashion the Erinyes offer a prayer for good civic conduct among the citizens, founded upon reciprocity, not blow for blow but blessing for blessing. Athenians are to "pay back to each other joy in return for joy" (984). The blessings promised by the converted Erinyes are "good things" and call for the disposition to return good for good:

εἴη δ' ἀγαθῶν
ἀγαθὴ διάνοια πολίταις

May the disposition of the citizens
be good, a return for good things.

Eum. 1012–13

The two types of blessings, the vegetative and the civic, are linked through the gods: Good behavior earns divine blessing and prosperity. In the language of the old order of the Erinyes, this was represented by the profit to be gained from fear and groaning (517–21). In the new order, fear and anger will continue to play a part (476, 690–95), but the powers the order serves are secular, those of a human collectivity sitting in judgment.

Despite Athena's careful preservation of the old vocabulary, it is the conversion of punishment into *charis* that dominates the end of the play. Accepting a home in the cave beneath the Areopagus, seat of the new court, the Erinyes offer a prayer for the sun's bounty to make Athens prosper (925–26). Vested in bright robes, they are conducted to their cave with the expectation that their goodwill will issue in prosperity (1028–31). Aeschylus' portrayal of the conversion of the Erinyes has been described as a "burlesque" (Rosenmeyer 1982, 355–66), a "standard mythical metamorphosis" (Reinhardt 1949, 156) and a "religious idea, awful, dark, and intensely satisfying" (Verrall 1908, xliii). What is clear is that it follows the traditional sequence in ritual appropriate for chthonic deities: (i) fear, (ii) actions of appeasement, (iii) blessings. Vengeance was the religious antithesis of *charis*, but one had no meaning without the other. Thus, we commonly find in Greek, as in other forms of primitive religion, contrary deities emerging from the same source or receiving the same sacrificial rituals.[18]

Aeschylus may have been indulging in some religious syncretism at the end of the *Oresteia*, which led to the identification of the converted Erinyes with the Eumenides or the Semnai Theai, an identification that would suit his dramatic, and possibly his political, purposes.[19] But such syncretism was common with chthonic powers. Maiden triads

[18] Burkert 1985, 202.

[19] At the time the *Oresteia* was produced, the court of the Areopagus was the center of controversy in Athens, having just been stripped of its special powers. Commentators differ on the extent to which Aeschylus was joining one side or the other of the political issue by his account of the founda-

of fertility goddesses went under several names although they presided over roughly the same functions. The Charites, one of these triads, were not infrequently addressed as *semnai* (Ch. 3 above). The Erinyes may never have actually become "Eumenides" in the play that bears the name,[20] but they display the contrasting powers common to underworld divinites, who are alternately angered and appeased. The bloodthirsty quest for vengeance at the beginning of the *Eumenides* is balanced by gentleness and fructifying peace at the end of the play. But the polarity does not pull apart at the middle. Fear, which dominates the dark side of chthonic chiaroscuro, remains; the chthonic goddesses still abide under the earth. But the dark side of chthonic *dikê* is potentially white, and when *dikê* is brought into the light of reason, something new has happened. Old *dikê* was the negative correlate of *charis*. Under the new order, in human hands with divine endorsement, it has become a *charis*. The goddesses inhabit Athenian soil; their power is no longer otherworldly but is bestowed upon Athenian citizens who have taken on themselves the responsibility for social restraint. Although the goddesses are not called Charites, they confer *charis* on Athens and leave for their new home calling out the significant words of *charis*-farewell, *chairete, chairete* (1014).

---

tion of the court in the play. See Dover 1957, 230–37; Podlecki 1966, 80–94; Dodds 1960, 19–31; and MacLeod 1982b, 127–33.

[20] Most modern commentators agree that the Erinyes received a new name in some lines that dropped out after 1027, but few would argue with Hermann that this name was the Eumenides. The name occurs in the hypothesis that was later assigned to the play, and the play may always have been referred to by this name (see Lloyd-Jones 1990, 209). The title "Eumenides," however, was probably not applied to the goddesses beneath the Areopagus hill before c. 410 B.C.E. (Sommerstein 1989, 11–12 and *ad loc.*) A much more likely identification in Aeschylus' mind was with the Semnai Theai, primitive earth-deities who inhabited a cave near the hill. The converted Erinyes are addressed as Σεμναί at the end of the play (1041). Later tradition associated them with oaths, prayers on behalf of Athens, and the judgments handed down by the Areopagus. For a fuller discussion of the Semnai Theai, see Lloyd-Jones, ibid., and A. L. Brown 1984, 260–81.

Chapter Eight

CONCLUSION

THIS BOOK began with the question, What is the link between the various and disparate meanings of *charis* in the archaic and early classical age of Greece? The inquiry, historical and discursive, began with the idea of *charis* as a social pleasure. The poetry showed, however, that the accent was placed on the element of reciprocity, on the obligation created by the giving of social pleasure to give social pleasure back, in return. The element of reciprocity sometimes takes such prominence, in fact, that the notion of social *favors* retreats and *charis* comes to mean vengeance (and *its* pleasures). In all of this it becomes clear that *charis* was a cardinal item in the moral system of the Greeks of the archaic and early classical age: It was the moral glue of their society, linking such other central moral ideas as *timê*, *dikê*, *themis*, *xenia*, and *aidôs*. This is a striking difference from our own ethical system in which grace and graciousness are laudable but not altogether necessary moral qualities—icing on the cake of rights and duties—belonging to manners rather than morals.

One version of *charis*, however, does not seem to be straightforwardly captured by this explanatory net: the *charis* of charm, beauty, allurement. How does it connect with favors of the battlefield, with reciprocal obligation, with the carefully calibrated regimen of exchange?

Both types of *charis* appear in the *Iliad*. Hera uses *charis* to seduce Zeus, and Achilles demands return-*charis* for his contribution to the Greek army. The clue to the common ingredient is also found in epic, in the *Odyssey*. Odysseus' *charis*-unction in Book 8 has as its intent the transformation of the hero from a dangerous outsider to a friend among the Phaeacians, and the result is that *aidôs* is aroused in them so that they welcome the stranger (21–22). With *charis* Athena removes the natural barriers that separate people who are unknown to each other, who might be experienced as a threat. *Charis* induces a social softening between strangers, friends, lovers, mortals, and gods. This experience, profoundly social, one of the best experiences known to humankind, is pleasurable. With death, social interchange is no longer possible: *Charis* cannot operate. When erotic *charis* has no personal object, when it is directed at mere facsimiles of the beloved—as when Menelaus looked at statues of Helen—the experience is hollow and empty, a ghost-*charis*. The eyes of lovers connect with each other, conduits of the love light that binds the two in each other's presence. With the *charis* of reciprocity, *aidôs* achieves this effect. Like the experience of a divine epiphany, which connects the beholder and the beheld through the action of *aidôs* with *charis*, these two qualities maintain social stability at large, binding individuals in the social fabric through mutual respect. Acts of kindness on the part of kings assure them of reverential *charis* from their subjects. Wonder and awe issue from the *charis* of good behavior, just as a beautiful woman or man radiates *charis* and provokes astonishment.

But, as Hesiod and Theognis complain, *aidôs* and *charis* are not durable phenomena. Social relationships are never static, and when these particular features disappear in the larger social sphere, there is cause for alarm. When a relationship between individuals is fractured by a loss of *charis* and *aidôs*, there is pain instead of pleasure. But the very transience of *charis* can heighten the pleasure taken in it. The *charis* of a young girl's *hôra* is all the more compelling and irresistible for its being confined to that brief period of the *akmê* of her youth. The bittersweet *charis*-pleasure that Theognis takes in the poignant moment arising from love's vicissitudes, when he is caught between pleasure and pain, is all the more intense for its being short-lived. *Charis* is to be found in the instability itself.

The transient nature of *charis*, in all its aspects, indeed of human pleasure of all kinds, was a fundamental tenet of the archaic world-view, where one's rise with good fortune was believed to be commensurate with one's imminent and inevitable fall from grace. Receiving the blessing of Charis was but a prelude to the loss of such favor, whether it was bestowed by some divinity, a friend or a lover. Momentarily, mortals and gods, friends and lovers, enjoyed the pleasure-bond established by *charis*, in the form of favors and kindnesses, or of human beauty and the gifts of love. The *charis* of love would naturally lead to the *charis* of a favor-exchange. Such a pleasure-bond, while subject to the inconstancy of fate and human frailty, was based on more than sexual gratification.

The precariousness of the duration of *charis*-pleasure was a common feature, then, of the two basic modes of its manifestation, which also shared the disposition to dissolve the natural barriers that separated individuals, in the early Greek world as now. But what we sense as two different kinds of *charis* may not have been seen as such by the archaic Greek mind. Beauty was an equally valid concept in ethics and aesthetics: Semonides' good bee-woman radiates *charis* and attracts admirers. In epinician poetry, *charis* transforms the glorious athlete in his moment of victory, winning for him the *aidôs* of spectators. But he also becomes an attractive prospect for a husband. And the fluidity of the aesthetic/ethical dimensions of *charis*, with its multivalent potential, outlived the archaic age, surviving in Theocritus' sixteenth *Idyll*, where the Charites refer at once to beautiful goddesses, glorifying poems, and the rewards anticipated by the poet in return for his *charis*.

Charis is, then, an adornment of social relationships or moral qualities—gold on silver, as Homer said, or the icing on the cake, as we might say. But as adornment it is functional, not superfluous and merely decorative. The pleasure of *charis* is the spur to social activity, the engine of morality, the reward of altruism. And *we* may still ask ourselves, in light of this, whether it isn't the icing that draws us to the cake.

Appendix 1

EURIPIDEAN *CHARIS*

THE *ORESTEIA* was produced in 458 B.C.E. Twenty-seven years later, in 431 B.C.E., Pericles delivered the famous funeral oration; its purpose was ostensibly to honor those who had fallen in the war with Sparta, but in reality it was an apologia for Athenian imperialism. In the midst of the speech Pericles says:

οὐ γὰρ πάσχοντες εὖ, ἀλλὰ δρῶντες κτώμεθα τοὺς φίλους. βε-
βαιότερος δὲ ὁ δράσας τὴν χάριν ὥστε ὀφειλομένην δι᾽ εὐνοίας ᾧ
δέδωκε σᾐζειν· ὁ δὲ ἀντοφείλων ἀμβλύτερος, εἰδὼς οὐκ ἐς
χάριν, ἀλλ᾽ ἐς ὀφείλημα τὴν ἀρετὴν ἀποδώσων.

It is not by receiving favors but by conferring them that we gain friends. The doer of *charis* is more secure, knowing that gratitude is owed to one who offers protection. But the one who owes us a favor is less enthusiastic, knowing that it is not as a return-favor but as a debt that he is repaying our service.

Thucydides 2.40

In Thucydides' version of the speech, we can see that *charis* has taken on new meaning, reflecting the dramatic change in social conventions which took place during the mid fifth century B.C.E. The reciprocity inherent in the practice of *charis*, the expectation that favors will be returned, is manipulated for political gain. The imperial power confers *charis* on its client-states in the knowledge that this will ensure their indebtedness. Thucydides' vocabulary preserves the asymmetry of the relationship: The donor partner is the member who is "more secure," whereas the indebted one, conscious of what he owes, is "duller," a "less keen" partner. Gone is Pindar's world, where client and patron lead and love each other in turns (*Pyth.* 10.65).

It was not only the war that brought about this change, a war in which Athens fought as an imperial power for the first time and imposed her designs upon smaller, weaker states. It was also the effect of an intellectual movement afoot, which called into question the very foundations upon which the commonest social conventions had rested. The effects of this challenge began to be felt in the plays of Aeschylus, but in Euripides we find the debate over the relativism of social conventions reaching a level that is at once more subtle and more intense. The sophists argued that these conventions were human, not divine, constructs and varied with time and place. The *charis*-exchange, as a strictly human practice, no longer had an external, absolute point of reference which would preserve the symmetry of the exchange. The sharpening of the rhetorical skills of these individuals who fell under the influence of the sophistic movement allowed them to argue for the justice of their personal claims in order to obtain some private advantage. They had recourse to principles that could be verbally manipulated for personal gain. As the appearance of a thing could belie the reality that lay beneath, so a semblance of justice could supplant real justice by the art of persuasion. *Logos* (speech) reigned, and did so without being morally aligned to any absolute principles.

As is clear from a study of the *Oresteia*, the moral complexity of the new order was not lost on the tragedians. Competitions between protagonists exploited the new moral relativism for dramatic effect. Clytemnestra makes claims on behalf of *charis* which are answered by the chorus' charge that this is a non-*charis*. In this debate, the pain suffered by the House of Atreus and by those struggling to make sense of this pain is laid bare. In the plays of Euripides, the subtlety of the *charis*-debates makes it more difficult to assess the competing claims. In addition, Euripides makes much greater use of the argument that *charis* can be detached from a reciprocal bond, and also from reality itself. The new relativism extended to perception: What one person perceived as *charis* another perceived as non-*charis*, an illusion, a fake. Wherein lies the reality? This is the enigma that Euripides has left us.

In the *Alcestis* the principal characters all perform acts intended to generate *charis*, but which produce more pain than pleasure. The one great act of *charis* in the play, the rescue of Alcestis from the underworld, is the result of behavior that can only be described as an act of non-*charis*. In the opening dialogue between Apollo and Thanatos, Apollo asks the Death-god for the *charis* of sparing the life of Alcestis.[1] When his request is refused, Apollo prophesies that Thanatos will perform the favor in any case, without any *charis* of good feeling; indeed, he will do it in anger (70–71). The favor of rescuing Alcestis will happen as a non-favor, performed in a spirit of resentment. Gone is the reciprocal advantage of *charis*, the easy flow of goodwill. One no longer expects a balanced social exchange.

Alcestis had offered her own death as a supreme sacrifice for her husband. This was a *charis* that Admetus' own parents had refused him. They were unwilling to exchange this favor for the *aidôs* that their son had shown them (659–61). But the favor presented by Alcestis to her husband is, in his eyes, an illusion, no favor. Despite appearances, her fate in dying was more pleasurable than that of her husband who was saved, for she was spared the bitterness of the solitude he suffered (935–61). But in Alcestis' view, this was a real *charis*, indeed a favor greater than could ever be recipro-

---

[1] The chain of *charis*-favors had begun earlier, when Apollo had rewarded Admetus for his kind reception during the god's enforced stay at the king's palace. In the first instance, the reciprocal favor had amounted to Apollo's making a deal with the Fates, such that the death of Admetus could be postponed if a substitute were found. Now that the substitute has turned out to be Alcestis, the favor risks losing its *charis* unless the queen can be saved. On the connection between *charis* and hospitality in the play, and the paradoxical treatment of this theme, see Conacher 1988, 37, 42–43.

cated (299). She asked only one thing in return, that Admetus not supplant her with a new wife (300–310). Admetus readily complies with her request, adding to this the promise that he will keep the house free from revelry of any sort (343–46). This last promise he breaks immediately after her death, when he admits Heracles into the house. Unwilling to turn the hero away, Admetus refuses Heracles' request for the *charis* of finding lodging for him elsewhere, when the royal house is obviously in mourning (544). Admetus disguises the fact that it is the queen's death that has caused this, so Heracles proceeds to outdo all guests who had preceded him in the degree of his merrymaking (747–62). This breach of the agreement reciprocating Alcestis' supreme *charis* (that was not a *charis*) leads to the ultimate *charis*, the one requested by Apollo and refused by Thanatos, the final rescuing of Alcestis from death. Heracles, repentant when he learns the truth about the death in the house, is determined to carry out the *charis* of restoring Alcestis (840–42, 1072–74).

But just as Admetus had hidden the real loss of his wife, so Heracles disguises her real return and presents the king with a woman fully veiled, whose identity he conceals. The woman appears to present a direct violation of the *charis*-contract with Alcestis, for she will be a replacement wife in a new marriage (1087). Heracles presses her into the personal keeping of Admetus, asking his trust, for soon it will be clear to him that this is the *charis* that he needs (1101). For Admetus to receive the woman is for him to grant a favor to Heracles, in return for an act intended as *charis*-pleasure for Admetus but experienced as no pleasure (1108). When Admetus accepts the woman and recognizes her identity, she becomes the ultimate *charis*, the final link in the chain. But this final *charis* is unreciprocal and ironic: Admetus is the one who has consistently denied *charis* to his wife.

The *Helen* also involves a dialectic on the *charis*, or lack of it, between husband and wife, but with a different emphasis. From sophistic discourse Euripides adapts the popular debate on the nature of *dikê* and on the extent to which illusion can be distinguished from reality. *Charis* provides some striking examples of the new relativity of justice and creates some splendid ironic passages in a play riddled with confusion over what is false or only apparent, and what is real.

In a rhetorical *agôn* that is crucial for her survival, Helen in Egypt tries to persuade Theonöe, the daughter of Helen's (now deceased) guardian, King Proteus, to conceal from her brother the fact of Menelaus' arrival from Troy. The brother, Theoclymenus, is anticipating marriage to Helen and would quickly get rid of the shipwrecked and weary former husband. Theonöe is faced with a difficult choice. Being honest with her brother is doing him a favor but, as Helen reminds her, in this case the *charis* of truthfulness does not follow the dictates of *dikê*: It undermines the "just" intent of her father who sheltered Helen, and it would be awarded to a brother who is "unjust" (917–23).

Helen continues with a suppliant plea to Theonöe to award the *charis* to her instead, a *charis* that is still wedded to *dikê* (940–41). Helen's position is that King Proteus had behaved justly in sheltering her during the Trojan War and that his children should do the same. The association of *charis* and *dikê* is a familiar one, but Helen adds a new gloss on the situation where *charis* (that of truthfulness) is divorced from *dikê*; in this it resembles the non-*charis* of the *Oresteia*. Detached from morality, such *charites* can be bought; these are "base" (900–902).

This is a new mood from that of the *Oresteia*. *Charis* does not cease to be itself, to become a non-*charis*, ignoring *dikê*; it just becomes bad. *Charis*, cornerstone of moral behavior in archaic Greece, is now in itself morally neutral and potentially evil, a commodity that can be bought for partisan purposes. As Helen argued on the basis of her interests, so Theoclymenus could presumably have demanded *charis* from his sister on the basis of kin-loyalty and honesty. But Theonöe is a seer with a high regard for piety (901, 919) and honor before the gods, and we sense that when she is won over by the appeals of Helen and Menelaus she is getting confirmation for her choice (to refuse *charis* to her brother) from the gods. She concludes that a *charis* for her brother would amount to bringing pollution upon herself. This stain would bring her dishonor in the eyes of the gods (1000– 1001).

The antithesis between illusion and reality, common in rhetorical speech, permeates the *Helen*. Theonöe can do her brother a real favor, while appearing to withhold one. By remaining silent about Menelaus' arrival, she will do him the favor of converting his impiety to piety (1017, 1020–21).

The contrast between reality and illusion presents many opportunities for dramatic irony in the play, and nowhere more successfully than in the scene where Theoclymenus is presented with the news of the (fictitious) death of Menelaus and with the request for a cenotaph-burial at sea. In reply to the news, Theoclymenus claims to take no *charis*-pleasure in the report, although he realizes his good fortune (1197). His anticipated good luck is of course marriage to Helen, easier to accomplish with evidence of her husband's death. But naturally neither the death nor his good fortune are real, any more than is his pretence at feeling no *charis*-pleasure in the news of Menelaus' death. This pretence is only a shadow, however, of the real deception being carried out by Helen. She invites Theoclymenus to prepare their wedding rites while she carries out the funerary rites for Menelaus. Delighted, he asks her what terms she requires, what *charis* he can provide in return for the *charis* of enjoying her as his wife (1234).

The reciprocal *charis* in marriage, known to Homer (*Il.* 11.243) and so memorably expressed by Tecmessa (*Ajax* 522), has grimmer overtones here. The real *charis* of marriage is being reserved for Menelaus, disguised as a funerary-*charis* (1273, 1378). The irony intensifies as Theoclymenus promises to reward the now-presumed dead Menelaus for his marriage-*charis* to Helen, by enabling her to carry out the death rites. This favor is, of course, the real *charis* Helen was ultimately seeking: the means of escape (1281). Theoclymenus becomes nervous when he realizes that the *charis* of Helen's feelings for her dead husband may incline her to drown herself and join him (1397), but Helen ignores the reference to the *charis* of conjugal love and assures him that it is no *charis*-favor to the dead to join them in death (1402). She returns to a request for *charis* from Theoclymenus, asking for a ship so that she may enjoy his *charis* "in full measure" (1411). We realize that her enjoyment entails taking away with her all his *charis* with the ship, not just his generosity but his anticipated pleasure in her. Her satisfaction with this favor will match the intensity of his expectations, but there will be no trace of reciprocity in her actions. She sustains his anticipation of this, however, with a promise full of ambiguity, saying, "This day will reveal to you my *charis*" (1420). We know, of course, that the wedding understood by Theoclymenus to be the return-favor for his *charis* is as hollow as the cenotaph of Menelaus, and his *charis* is as empty of fulfilment as it promised to be full (1411). The real *charis* belongs to Menelaus, uninterrupted enjoyment of Helen, for which he prays to Zeus as he leaves the stage (1449–50). This is piety rewarded. Ultimately, the *charis* of good fortune comes to him, as it was denied to his impious rival. Menelaus and Helen are the winners in the sophistic *agôn* of the play. Her adroitness in manipulating the *logos* has earned them rightful *charis*. But, interestingly enough, there are traditional elements in the *charis* that has prevailed in the end. It is reciprocal and a gift from the gods.

The power of persuasion that motivated rhetorical speech is relentlessly exercised in Euripides' *Hecuba*, where the object is not salvation but death and revenge. A remnant of Greek heroes from the Trojan War was detained in Thrace with their Trojan captives, their ships halted by lack of winds. The ghost of Achilles has stilled the winds, demanding the sacrifice of the Trojan princess Polyxena as a grave offering, his final reward. The smooth-talking Odysseus, "honey-tongued *charis*-pleaser of the *dêmos*" (132), persuades his reluctant comrades to comply. Otherwise, he says, they will be charged with a "lack of *charis*-gratitude" by the Greek soldiers who, like Achilles, fought and died in the war (138–40).

When Odysseus confronts the mother of the proposed

victim, Queen Hecuba, he meets her counterclaim for a *charis*, an act of gratitude he owes her. Anxious to save her daughter, Hecuba assails demagogues like Odysseus, a "thankless race in pursuit of honor" (254–55). On the grounds that she had saved Odysseus' life while he was in Troy (249–50), she asks for a return-*charis*, she a suppliant now as he had been then (272–76). Odysseus interprets his return obligation as quid pro quo, promising only to spare her life. Polyxena, however, must die, he says, because of the higher claim of Achilles to *charis*, the *charis* of honor, or *timê*; only her death will satisfy him for eternity (309–20).

In Odysseus' words we see that *charis* has become a political expedient. Showing *charis* to the honorable dead over reciprocating the *charis* of individual living benefactors is a mechanism for keeping men dying nobly for the state. Odysseus adds the vaunt that this type of *charis* is the mark of superior civilization. The Trojans, barbarians, do not carry as high a respect for the heroic dead (328–30).

Hecuba, who bases her claims on personal, not political allegiance, has lost round 1 of the *agôn*. Polyxena dies, and the queen's anguish is doubled when news reaches her of the death of her son Polydorus, who had been sent to the Thracian King Polymestor with some Trojan gold for safe-keeping during the war. Desperate, she tries to collect a return favor from Agamemnon. She begs him to seek revenge for this murder, a favor he owes her for the sexual favors he has enjoyed with another of her daughters, Cassandra. Hecuba asks for *charis* in Cassandra's name, a return for the nocturnal *charis* Agamemnon enjoyed with her (830–32).

Hecuba has the right to claim *charis* in Cassandra's stead. As her mother she has the right to reciprocal advantage for the effort of rearing her daughter. Agamemnon recognizes this and is sympathetic to her call for the *charis* of revenge taken upon Polymestor. The Thracian king had violated the laws of guest-friendship, *xenia*. But Agamemnon is loath to be seen as a visible accomplice in this act, "for the *charis* of Cassandra"(855–56). Although here *charin* functions as a preposition ("for the sake of Cassandra"), the erotic undercurrent is unmistakable. Agamemnon recognizes the political power of sexual *charis*. Hecuba laments his base political oversensitivity (864–67) as she had that of Odysseus; her reference points are governed not by public image but by personal allegiance and the need to punish evil (845). But she complies with the "more civilized" posture assumed by the Greek king and decides to take revenge alone, asking one thing only of Agamemnon, that he stop his troops if they attempt to rescue Polymestor. Hecuba releases Agamemnon from having to appear to feel *charis*-loyalty to her as mother of Cassandra (874).

Agamemnon complies with her request. The irony intensifies, as it did in the *Helen*, when the central deed of deception occurs. Polymestor, lured by Hecuba to her tents with his two young sons, addresses her and the deceased Priam as "dearest" (952) and sympathizes with the sudden reversals of Trojan fortune (953–61). After this ominous preamble, he asks what need she has of him, what help he can offer to a friend (976, 984–86). Hecuba ironically asks of him "befriended by her as she is by him" (1000) to keep the gold and jewels that she has brought from Troy and secreted in the women's tents. When the king enters the tents, Hecuba and the Trojan women carry out the revenge, killing the king's sons and stabbing out his eyes with brooch-pins. The wounded and grieving Polymestor gives an account of this to Agamemnon, while justifying his murder of Polydorus. This had been a *charis* for the Greeks, he says, for he had destroyed one of their enemies (1175–76). Hecuba intercedes with a verbal riposte that cross-examines Polymestor's words: "Just what was this *charis* that you were in eager haste to deliver?" (1202–03).

Now arguing from the political, not the personal, vantage point, Hecuba adapts the rhetorical tools of Odysseus and argues that Polymestor, a barbarian, should never be seen to be a friend of the "civilized" Greeks (1200–1201). His real intent was not other-directed, but base and personal. If he were really a friend of the Greeks, why did he not kill her son when Troy had had the upper hand and was a threat to the Greeks? Only then would getting rid of the young prince in his care have been a legitimate *charis* for Agamemnon and earned his gratitude (1211–13). Polymestor's actions carry more weight than do his words, says Hecuba; rhetoric must never make base actions appear to be good (1188–92). If one were persuaded by the Thracian's speech, one would be showing favor to a host who is impious and unjust, taking *charis*-pleasure in what is wicked (1236–37).

With these words, Hecuba wins the final round of the rhetorical *agôn*, persuading Agamemnon of the baseness of Polymestor, not only because he murdered her son but because he violated the laws of *xenia*. Hecuba, like Helen, uses rhetorical tricks and adapts them to her personal needs. But her actions, unlike those of her honey-tongued mentor, are wedded, as is Helen's appeal to Theonöe, to the traditional pattern that requites good with good. This pattern refuses to detach such requital from the *dikê* that is at once personal and universal, that redresses the balance by returning favors to a benefactor and by punishing an evildoer. It is worth noting that Euripides, thoroughly versed in the rhetoric of his time and the moral relativism it purveyed, gives the final word to traditional morality and to women.

Appendix 2

THE PREPOSITIONAL USE OF χάριν

A T *Il.*15.744 we can see the foundation for the later use of χάριν as a preposition. With χάριν Ἕκτορος ὀτρύναντος (the *charis* of Hector rousing his troops), the word χάριν, a noun (accusative) in apposition, is on its way to acquiring the meaning "for the sake of," which it acquires at a later stage. An interim stage will be the adverbial accusative or quasi-preposition. At this point, however, it is practically synonymous with χαριζόμενος, or φέρων χάριν Ἕκτορι δίῳ, *Il.*5.211, and retains the significance of the noun χάρις.

Hesiod, at *Op.* 709, writes μηδὲ ψεύδεσθαι γλώσσης χάριν (Don't lie, with the *charis* of your tongue). Some translators have given the word χάριν prepositional force here, producing a translation that is not inappropriate ("Don't lie by grace of [i.e., with] your tongue"). But the prepositional use of χάριν, which retains little of the original semantic color of the word, does not occur regularly until later (see West 1978, *ad loc.*, who translates γλώσσης χάριν as "a grace consisting of mere words"). Other texts that connect γλῶσσα and (the nonprepositional) χάρις are cited by Fränkel 1975, 128n.6. The susceptibility of both γλῶσσα and χάρις to πειθώ, the power of persuasion, makes the association of the two words a natural one. The power of the tongue to please is expressed by the ritual cry εὐφημεῖτε, and by the Roman cautionary words *favete linguis* found in Horace's *Odes* 3.2.1. (For parallel passages in Greek and Latin literature, see Smith 1913, 394.) In attempting to get at the meaning of the Hesiodic passage, West 1978 cites *Il.* 7.351–52, ὅρκια πιστὰ ψευσάμενοι, where Antenor points out that the Greek warriors have perjured themselves. This oxymoron, combining lying with trustworthiness, is a useful parallel to *Op.* 709, in that it underscores the fact that, as one expects ὅρκια to be πιστά, so everyone recognizes that words from the tongue have the capacity to please (and therefore show χάρις).

A good example of χάριν functioning as an appositive comes from Semonides:

ἀνὴρ δ᾿ ὅταν μάλιστα θυμηδεῖν δοκῇ
κατ᾿ οἶκον, ἢ θεοῦ μοῖραν ἢ ἀνθρώπου χάριν

Whenever a man seems to be especially enjoying himself
at home, a dispensation sent by a god or a favour from a
fellow-man

Semonides 7.103–4

In this passage μοῖραν and χάριν are syntactically parallel. Given that μοῖρα does not evolve into a preposition, both must be taken as appositives, explaining the verb θυμηδεῖν. A double apposition is also found in Pindar's *Fifth Pythian* Ode (102), where ὄλβον and χάριν represent the act of listening to the victory celebration (see above, Ch. 6).

In Pindar's *Third Pythian* Ode, the reversal of the royal house of Thebes from a state of suffering to success is expressed as Διὸς δὲ χάριν (a *charis* of Zeus, 95). Commentators have regularly taken χάριν here as a preposition, "thanks to." For example, see Gildersleeve 1890 *ad loc.* and Bury 1890 *ad Nem.* 1.5–6. Maehler 1982 *ad* 9.97 takes it as an adverbial accusative. The transition from sorrow to joy is an occasion that would naturally be called a χάρις, such as we find with the victor's exchanging his πόνος for victory, and keeping this force in this instance reinforces the fact that ultimately it is a gift of the gods. The following passage from Bacchylides may be cited as parallel to the Διὸς δὲ χάριν of *Pyth.* 3:

Κλεοπτολέμῳ δὲ χάριν
νῦν χρὴ Ποσειδᾶνός τε Πετρ[αι-
ου τέμενος κελαδῆσαι
Πυρρίχου τ᾿ εὔδοξον ἱππόνικ[ον υἱόν

Now, as a *charis* for Kleoptolemus,
it is right to celebrate the sacred precinct

of Poseidon Petraios,
and the glorious son of Pyrrichus, victor in the chariot race.

Bacchylides 14.19–21

χάριν stands in apposition to the verbal phrase νῦν
χρὴ . . . κελαδῆσαι (see Jebb 1905 *ad loc.*, Maehler 1982 *ad
loc.*, and Gerber 1984 *ad loc.*). The identical construction is
found in Pindar's *Tenth Olympian*:

> καί νυν ἐπωνυμίαν χάριν
> νίκας ἀγερώχου κελαδησόμεθα βροντάν
> καὶ πυρπάλαμον βέλος
> ὀρσικτύπου Διός

> Now, as namesake *charis* of the mighty victory,
> let us celebrate the thunder
> and the fire-wrought weapon
> of thunder-rousing Zeus

Pindar Ol. 10.78–81

Pindar goes on to say, as if explaining the apposition, that
the fiery thunderbolt is a fitting emblem for the victory (82–
83). Yet another Pindaric parallel is found at *Pyth.* 11.9–12,
where κελαδήσετ᾽ takes (as above) a double object and the
whole is represented by χάριν.

This appositive χάριν is also found in Bacchylides' fifth
ode (χρὴ] δ᾽ ἀλαθείας χάριν αἰνεῖν, 187–88). Here it stands
for the verbal injunction "one must praise." Translating
χάριν as a preposition (Jebb 1905 *ad loc.*, for example) has
the ring of the gratuitous, and taking it in apposition to
αἰνεῖν gives it the centrality it merits: "one must praise, a
charis of *alatheia*."

"As a *charis* for" or "as tribute to," the appositive interpretation, differs but little in sense from the prepositional
translation "for the glory of," "for the sake of." But the noun
in apposition retains more of the concreteness of χάρις.
Given the rich associations of the word in epinician contexts, I prefer to opt for the noun-in-apposition wherever it
is not excluded on philological grounds. Making the choice

can, of course, be as arbitrary as deciding that a once color-
ful phrase has become a dead metaphor.

There is one passage in Bacchylides for which the case for
noun-in-apposition is difficult to make:

> ὃς δὲ μυ-
> ρία μὲν ἀμφιπολεῖ φρενί,
> τὸ δὲ παρ' ἀμάρ τε ⟨καὶ⟩ νύκτα μελλόντων
> χάριν αἰὲν ἰάπτεται
> κέαρ, ἄκαρπον ἔχει πόνον.

But he who busies himself with countless cares in his mind
and is always wounded in his heart by day and by night,
owing to the *charis* of the future,
has fruitless toil.

Bacchylides fr. 11.3–5

The thought is similar to that found in Pindar's *Tenth Pythian*, 62–63, *Olympian* 1.99, and *Third Pythian*, 3.62: One
should concentrate on the things at hand, things that are
manageable. Although χάριν in Bacchylides fr. 11 functions
syntactically as a preposition or adverbial accusative, it
probably retains some of the usual semantic content of
χάρις, "goodness," "blessing" etc. The usual translation
"for the sake of the future" does not do justice to the proverbial nature of the sentiment found here: Bacchylides is advising that one should concentrate on the goods at hand,
not the prospect of good things to come.

GLOSSARY*

agathoi (ἀγαθοί) — the good class of people for Theognis; the aristocrats

agôn (ἀγών) — competition, athletic contest

aidôs (αἰδώς) — sense of reverence, awe; the power to instill this sense

aglaia (ἀγλαΐα) — brilliance

alatheia (ἀλάθεια) — truth, unveiling

apoina (ἄποινα) — ransom, price paid in compensation

aretê (ἀρετή) — courage, valor, excellence

bia (βία) — physical force

chairein (χαίρειν) — to rejoice

chara (χαρά) — joy, delight

charin oida; charin eidenai (χάριν οἶδα, χάριν εἰδέναι) — I know the favor, I thank; to know the favor, to thank

deiloi (δειλοί) — the people without social graces for Theognis

dikê, dika (δίκη, δίκα) — justice, case before a tribunal

dôra (δῶρα) — gifts

eros (ἔρος) — love, passion

euphrosynê (εὐφροσύνη) — merriment, joy, especially at the feast

geras (γέρας) — gift of honor, privilege

hêbê (ἥβη) — youth, the prime of youth

hêdonê (ἡδονή) — delight, pleasure, instant gratification

hôra (ὥρα) — season, the prime of youth

hybris (ὕβρις) — arrogance, lack of respect for others

kakoi (κακοί) — the bad sort of people for Theognis, those without social graces

koinônia (κοινωνία) — communal fellowship

kommos (κομμός) — a lamentation for the dead, often involving loud rhythmic cries and beating of the breast

kômos (κῶμος) — a band of revelers, a festive procession, a regular part of the victory celebration

* This is not intended as a complete definition of each word, but as a reminder of the meaning given in the body of the text. The different dialects represented are true to the texts quoted.

lôbê (λώβη) — mutilation, outrage
logos (λόγος) — word, speech
moira (μοῖρα) — apportionment, share; fate
paideia (παιδεία) — moral and cultural instruction of the young
peithô (πειθώ) — persuasion
philia (φιλία) — friendship
pistis (πίστις) — faithfulness
poinê (ποινή) — penalty, requital payment
polis (πόλις) — city, city-state
sophos (σοφός) — wise, skilled, especially in poetry
sôphrosynê (σωφροσύνη) — sound-mindedness, moderation
thalia, thaliai (pl.) (θαλία, θαλίαι) — flourishing, abundance; festivities (pl.)
themis (θέμις) — established custom, right
thymos (θυμός) — the place in the body which was the source of the passions
timê (τιμή) — honor, price, worth
tinein (τίνειν) — to pay a penalty; to take vengeance
tisis (τίσις) — requital payment, recompense, retribution
xenia, xeinia (ξενία, ξεινία) — friendly gifts given by a host to a guest; the relationship between host and guest

BIBLIOGRAPHY

Adkins, A.W.H. "'Honour' and 'Punishment' in the Homeric Poems." *BICS* 7 (1960), 23–32.

———. "'Friendship' and 'Self-Sufficiency' in Homer and Aristotle." *CQ* n.s. 13 (1963), 30–45.

———. "εὔχομαι, εὐχωλή, εὖχος in Homer." *CQ* n.s. 19 (1969), 20–33.

———. "Threatening, Abusing and Feeling Angry in the Homeric Poems." *JHS* 84 (1969), 7–21.

———. *Merit and Responsibility — A Study in Greek Values*. Oxford, 1970.

———. "Homeric Values and Homeric Society." *JHS* 91 (1971), 1–14.

———. "Truth, κοσμός, and ἀρετή in Homer." *CQ* n.s. 22 (1972), 1–18.

———. *Moral Values and Political Behaviour in Ancient Greece: From Homer to the End of the Fifth Century*. New York, 1972.

———. review of E. A. Havelock, *The Greek Concept of Justice: From Its Shadow in Homer to Its Substance in Plato*. *CP* 75 (1980), 256–68.

———. "Values, Goals and Emotions in the *Iliad*." *CP* 77 (1982), 292–326.

Arieti, J. A. "Achilles' Guilt." *CJ* 80 (1985), 193–203.

Austin, Norman. "Idyll 16: Theocritus and Simonides." *TAPA* 98 (1967), 1–21.

Barrett, W. S., ed. *Euripides. Hippolytus*. Oxford, 1964.

Bassett, S. E. "The Ἁμαρτία of Achilles." *TAPA* 65 (1934), 47–69.

———. "God, Man and Animal." In *Greek Poetry and Philosophy: Studies in Honour of Leonard Woodbury*, ed. D. E. Gerber, Chico, Calif., 1984, 1–31.

Bell, John. "Κίμβιξ καὶ σοφός. Simonides in the anecdotal tradition." *QUCC* 28 (1978), 29–91.

Benveniste, E. *Le Vocabulaire des institutions indo-européennes*. 2 vols. Paris, 1969.

Bernardini, P. A. "La dike della lira e la dike dell' atleta (Pindaro, *P.* 1, 1–2; *O.* 9, 98)." *QUCC* n.s. 2 (1979), 79–85.

Bielohlawek, K. "Gastmahls- und Symposienslehren bei griechischen Dichtern." *WS* 58 (1940), 11–30.

Blech, M. *Studien zum Kranz bei den Griechen*. Berlin, 1982.

Blundell, M. W. *Helping Friends and Harming Enemies.* Cambridge/New York, 1989.

Bonanno, M. G. "Osservazioni sul tema della 'giusta' reciprocità amorosa da Saffo ai comici." *QUCC* 16 (1973), 110–20.

Borgeaud, W. A. "Le vigneron diluvial et le chasseur auroral— étude onomastique." *RBPh* 1 (1972), 30–43.

Borgeaud, W. A., and B. MacLachlan. "Les Kharites et la lumière." *RBPh* 63 (1985), 5–14.

Bowra, C. M. *Tradition and Design in the Iliad.* Oxford, 1930.

———. "Stesichorus in the Peloponnese." *CQ* 28 (1934), 115–19.

———. *Greek Lyric Poetry from Alcman to Simonides*[2]. Oxford, 1961.

———. *Pindar.* Oxford, 1964.

———., ed. *Pindari Carmina cum Fragmentis*[2]. Oxford, 1947.

Bremer, D. "Theia bei Pindar: Mythos und Philosophie." *A & A* 21 (1975), 85–96.

———. *Licht und Dunkel in der frühgriechischen Dichtung: Interpretationen zur Vorgeschichte der Lichtmetaphysik.* Bonn, 1976.

Brown, A. L. "Eumenides in Greek Tragedy." *CQ* 34 (1984), 260–81.

Brown, C. G. "The Bridegroom and the Athlete: The Proem to Pindar's Seventh Olympian." In *Greek Poetry and Philosophy: Studies in Honour of Leonard Woodbury,* ed. D. E. Gerber. Chico, Calif., 1984a, 37–50.

———. "Ruined by Lust: Anacreon Fr. 44 Gentili (432 *PMG*)." *CQ* 34 (1984b), 37–42.

———. "Anactoria and the Χαρίτων ἀμαρύγματα: Sappho fr. 16,18 Voigt." *QUCC* n.s. 32 (1989), 7–13.

———. "Honouring the Goddess: Philicus' Hymn to Demeter." *Aegyptus* 70 (1990), 173–89.

Buckler, John. "The Charitesia at Boiotian Orchomenos." *AJP* 105 (1984), 49–53.

Buffière, Félix. *Les Mythes d'Homère et la pensée grecque.* Paris, 1956.

Bundy, E. L. *Studia Pindarica. University of California Publications in Classical Philology.* (1962). Vol. I: "The Eleventh Olympian Ode," 1–34. Vol. II: "The First Isthmian Ode," 35–92. (= *Studia Pindarica.* Berkeley/Los Angeles, 1986).

Burkert, Walter. *Greek Religion.* Cambridge, Mass., 1985.

Burnett, A. P. *Three Archaic Poets: Archilochus, Alcaeus, Sappho.* Cambridge, Mass. 1983.

———. *The Art of Bacchylides.* Cambridge, Mass./London, 1985.

Bury, J. B., ed. *The Nemean Odes of Pindar.* London/New York, 1890.

————, ed. *The Isthmian Odes of Pindar*. London, 1892.

Bushala, E. W. "Συζύγιαι Χάριτες, *Hippolytus* 1147." *TAPA* 100 (1969), 23–29.

Buxton, R. G. A. *Persuasion in Greek Tragedy*. Cambridge, 1982.

Calame, Claude. *Les Choeurs de jeunes filles en Grèce archaïque*. Vol. I. Rome, 1977.

Calder, W. M. III. "Gold for Bronze: Iliad 6, 232–36." In *Studies Presented to Sterling Dow on His Eightieth Birthday*, ed. K. J. Rigsby. *GRBS* Monograph 10. Durham, N.C., 1984, 31–35.

Campbell, D. A. *Greek Lyric Poetry*. London, 1967.

Carne-Ross, D. S. "Three Preludes for Pindar." *Arion* 2 (1975), 160–92.

————. *Pindar*. New Haven/London, 1985.

Carrière, Jean. *Théognis de Mégare: Etude sur le recueil élégiaque attribué à ce poète*. Paris, 1948.

Carson, Anne. "The Burners: A Reading of Bacchylides' Third Epinician Ode." *Phoenix* 38 (1984), 111–19.

Chantraine, P. *Dictionnaire étymologique de la langue grecque*. Paris, 1968.

Ciani, Maria Grazia. *ΦΑΟΣ et termini affini nella poesia greca: Introduzione a una fenomenologia della luce*. Florence, 1974.

Clay, J. S. *The Wrath of Athena: Gods and Men in the Odyssey*. Princeton, 1983.

Coldstream, J. N. "Gift Exchange in the Eighth Century B.C." In *The Greek Renaissance of the Eighth Century B.C.*, ed. R. Hägg. Stockholm, 1983, 201–7.

Cole, Th. "Archaic Truth." *QUCC* n.s. 13 (1983), 7–28.

Compagner, R. "Reciprocità economica in Pindaro." *QUCC* n.s. 29 (1988), 77–93.

Conacher, D. J. *Euripidean Drama*. Toronto/London, 1967.

————. "Comments on an Interpretation of Aeschylus, *Agamemnon* 182–183." *Phoenix* 30 (1976), 328–36.

————. *Aeschylus' Prometheus Bound: a literary commentary*. Toronto, 1980.

————. "Rhetoric and Relevance in Euripidean Drama." *AJP* 102 (1981), 3–25.

————. "Structural Aspects of Euripides' *Alcestis*." In *Studies in Honour of Leonard Woodbury.*, ed. D. E. Gerber. Chico, Calif., 1984, 73–81.

————, ed. *Euripides. Alcestis*. Warminster, 1988.

Considine, P. "Some Homeric Terms for Anger." *AClass* 9 (1966), 15–25.

Cook, A. B. *Zeus: A Study in Ancient Religion*. Vol. I: *Zeus of the Bright Sky*. Cambridge, 1914.

Craig, J. D. "ΧΡΥΣΕΑ ΧΑΛΚΕΙΩΝ." *CR* n.s. 17 (1969), 243–45.

Crotty, K. *Song and Action: The Victory Odes of Pindar*. Baltimore, 1982.

Davies, M. "Alcman and the Lover as Suppliant." *ZPE* 64 (1986), 13–14.

Deichgräber, Karl. *Charis und Chariten, Grazie und Grazien*. Munich, 1971.

Denniston, J. D. *The Greek Particles*. Oxford, 1954.

———, and Denys Page, eds. *Aeschylus. Agamemnon*. Oxford, 1957.

Deonna, W. *Le Symbolisme de l'oeil*. Paris, 1965.

Detienne, M. *Les Maîtres de vérité dans la Grèce archaïque*. Paris, 1967.

Dodds, E. R. *The Greeks and the Irrational*. Berkeley/Los Angeles, 1951.

———. "Morals and Politics in the *Oresteia*." *PCPS* 186 (1960), 19–31.

———, ed. *Euripides. Bacchae²*. Oxford, 1960.

Donlan, W. "Scale, Value , and Function in the Homeric Economy." *AJAH* 6 (1981), 101–17.

———. "The politics of generosity in Homer." *Helios* 9, n.s. 2 (1982a), 1–15.

———. "Reciprocities in Homer." *CW* 75 (1982b), 137–75.

———. "The Unequal Exchange between Glaucus and Diomedes in Light of the Homeric Gift-Economy." *Phoenix* 43 (1989), 1–15.

Dornsieff, Franz. *Pindars Stil*. Berlin, 1921.

———. *Die archaïsche Mythenerzählung. Folgerungen aus dem homerischen Apollon hymnos*. Berlin/Leipzig, 1933.

Dover, K. "The Political Aspect of Aeschylus' *Eumenides*." *JHS* 77 (1957), 230–37. (Reprinted in his *Greek and the Greeks*. Oxford, 1987, 161–75).

———. "Eros and Nomos." *BICS* 44 (1964), 31–47.

———. *Greek Popular Morality in the Time of Plato and Aristotle*. Berkeley, 1974.

———. *Greek Homosexuality*. Cambridge, Mass., 1978.

———. "The Portrayal of Moral Evaluation in Greek Poetry." *JHS* 103 (1983), 35–48 (= *Greek and the Greeks*, 77–96).

Duchemin, Jacqueline. *Pindare, poète et prophète*. Paris, 1955.

Eichholz, D. E. "The Propitiation of Achilles." *AJP* 74 (1953), 137–48.

Evans, Elizabeth C. "Literary Portraiture in Ancient Epic: A Study of the Descriptions of Physical Appearance in Classical Epic." *HSCP* 58–59 (1948), 189–217.

Farnell, L. R. *The Cults of the Greek States*. 5 vols. Oxford, 1909.

———. *Critical Commentary on the Works of Pindar*. First printed in his *The Works of Pindar*, Vol. II: *Critical Commentary*. London, 1932.

Fernandes, R. M. R. "O Tema das Graças na Poesia Classica." Diss. Lisbon, 1962.

Finley, M. *The World of Odysseus*². New York, 1967. Second revised edition, 1978.

Fowler, Barbara Hughes. "The Archaic Aesthetic." *AJP* 105 (1984), 119–50.

Fraenkel, E., ed. Aeschylus. *Agamemnon*. 3 vols. Oxford, 1950.

Fränkel, H. "Pindars Religion." *Ant* 3 (1927), 39–63.

———. *Early Greek Poetry and Philosophy*. Oxford, 1975.

Franzmann, J. W. "The Early Development of the Greek Concept of Charis." Diss. University of Wisconsin, 1973.

Frisk, H. *Griechisches etymologisches Wörterbuch*. Heidelberg, 1960.

Fulda, Albert. *Untersuchungen über die Sprache der homerische Gedichte*. Dursburg, 1865.

Gallant, T. W. "Agricultural Systems, Land Tenure and the Reforms of Solon." *ABSA* 77 (1982), 111–24.

Garland, R. *The Greek Way of Death*. Ithaca, 1985.

Garvie, A. F., ed. *Aeschylus. Choephoroi*. Oxford/New York, 1986.

Gentili, B. "Verità e accordo contrattuale (σύνθεσις) in Pindaro, fr. 205 Sn. *ICS* 6 (1981), 215–20.

———. "La veneranda Saffo." *QUCC* 2 (1966), 37–62. (Reprinted in his *Poesia e pubblico nella Grecia antica*. Urbino, 1984, 285–94).

Gerber, D. E. "The Gifts of Aphrodite (Bacchylides 17.10)." *Phoenix* 19 (1965), 212–13.

———. *Pindar's Olympian One: A Commentary*. Toronto, 1982.

———. *Lexicon in Bacchylidem*. Zurich, 1984.

Gernet, L. "Frairies antiques." *REG* 41 (1928), 313–59.

———. "La notion mythique de le valeur en Grece." *Journal de psychologie normale et pathologique* 41 (1948), 415–62. In *The Anthropology of Ancient Greece*. Baltimore, 1981, 73–111.

Giacomelli, A. "The Justice of Aphrodite in Sappho Fr.1." *TAPA* 110 (1980), 135–42.

Gianotti, G. F. *Per una poetica Pindarica*. Turin/Paravia, 1975.

———. "Odi et Amo Ergo Sum." Diss. Toronto, 1981.

Gildersleeve, B. L., ed. *Pindar. The Olympian and Pythian Odes.* New York, 1890.

Gow, A. S. F., ed. *Theocritus.* 2 vols. Cambridge, 1950.

Griffin, J. *Homer on Life and Death.* Oxford, 1980.

Griffith, M., ed. *Aeschylus. Prometheus Bound.* Cambridge, 1983.

Groffridi, C. "Ὕβρις e Δίκη nell'arcaismo greco." *SDHI* 49 (1983), 331–36.

Gundert, H. *Pindar und sein Dichterberuf.* Frankfurt, 1935.

Haggerty Krappe, A. "Les Charites." *REG* 45 (1932), 155–62.

Halperin, D. "Plato and Erotic Reciprocity." *CA* 5 (1986), 60–80.

Hands, A. R. *Charities and Social Aid in Greece and Rome.* London/Ithaca, 1968.

Harrison, J. "Delphika." *JHS* 19 (1899), 205–51.

———. *Prolegomena to the Study of Greek Religion.* Cambridge, 1903.

———. *Themis: A Study of the Social Origins of Greek Religion.* Cambridge, 1912.

Havelock, E. A. *The Greek Concept of Justice.* Cambridge, Mass., 1978.

Herman, G. *Ritualized Friendship and the Greek City.* Cambridge, 1987.

Hewitt, J. W. "On the Development of the Thank-Offering among the Greeks." *TAPA* 43 (1912), 95–111.

———. "The Thank-Offering and Greek Religious Thought." *TAPA* 45 (1914), 77–90.

———. "Some Aspects of the Treatment of Ingratitude in Greek and English Literature." *TAPA* 48 (1917), 37–48.

———. "Gratitude and Ingratitude in the Plays of Euripides." *AJP* 43 (1922), 331–43.

———. "The Development of Political Gratitude." *TAPA* 55 (1924), 35–51.

———. "The Terminology of 'Gratitude' in Greek." *CP* 22 (1927), 142–61.

———. "Gratitude to Parents in Greek and Roman Literature." *AJP* 52 (1931), 30–48.

Hollis, A. S. *Callimachus. Hecale.* Oxford/New York, 1990.

Hope-Simpson, R., and J. F. Lazenby. *The Catalogue of Ships in Homer's Iliad.* Oxford, 1970.

Hudson-Williams, T., ed. *The Elegies of Theognis.* London, 1910.

Humphreys, S. *Anthropology and the Greeks.* London, 1978.

Irwin, E. "The Crocus and the Rose." In *Greek Poetry and Philosophy: Studies in Honour of Leonard Woodbury,* ed. D. E. Gerber. Chico, Calif., 1984, 147–68.

Jaeger, W. *Paideia: The Ideals of Greek Culture.* Vol. I². Oxford, 1945.

Jebb, R. C., ed. *Bacchylides. The Poems and Fragments.* Cambridge, 1905.

Kahn, Charles H. *Anaximander and the Origins of Greek Cosmologies.* New York/London, 1960.

―――. *The Verb 'Be' and Its Synonyms: Philosophical and Grammatical Studies,* ed. J. W. M. Verhaar. Foundations of Language Supplementary Series, Vol. XVI, Part 6. Boston: Dordrecht, 1973.

―――. "Anaximander's Fragment: The Universe Governed by Law." In *The Presocratics,* ed. A. P. D. Mourelatos. Garden City, N.Y., 1974, 99–117.

Kakridis, J. T. "Die 14 olympische Ode." *Serta Philologica Aenipontana* 3 (1979), 141–47.

Kardara, C. "ΕΡΜΑΤΑ ΤΡΙΓΛΕΝΤΑ ΜΟΡΟΕΝΤΑ." *AJA* 65 (1961), 62–65.

Kirk, G. S. *Homer and the Oral Tradition.* Cambridge, 1976.

Kirkwood, G. *Selections from Pindar.* Chico, Calif., 1982.

Knauss, J. *Wasserbau und Geschichte minyscher Epoche–bayerische Zeit (vier Jahrhunderte–ein Jahrzehnt).* Munich, 1990.

Komornicka, A. M. "Quelques remarques sur la notion d' ΑΛΑΘΕΙΑ et de ΨΕΥΔΟΣ chez Pindare." *Eos* 60 (1972), 235–53.

Koniaris, G. L. "On Sappho, Fr. 16 (LP)." *Hermes* 95 (1967), 257–68.

Kraus, T. *Hekate: Studien zu Wesen und Bild der Göttin in Kleinasien und Griechenland.* Heidelberg, 1960.

Kurke, L. *The Traffic of Praise: Pindar and the Poetics of Social Economy.* Ithaca, 1991.

Lanata, G. *Poetica pre-Platonica: testimonianze e frammenti.* Florence, 1963.

―――. "Sul linguaggio amoroso di Saffo." *QUCC* 2 (1966), 63–79.

Lasserre, F. "Ornements érotiques dans la poésie lyrique archaïque." In *Serta Turyniana,* ed. John L. Heller. Urbana, Ill., 1974, 5–33.

Latacz, Joachim. *Zum Wortfeld "Freude" in der Sprache Homers.* Heidelberg, 1966.

Latte, K. "De saltationibus capita quinque." Diss. Königsberg, Giessen, 1913.

Lavelle, B. M. "Archilochus Fr. 6 West and Ξενία." *CJ* 76 (1981), 197–99.

Lawler, Lillian B. *The Dance in Ancient Greece.* London, 1964.

Leaf, W., ed. *Homer. The Iliad.* 2 vols. London, 1886.

Lechat, H. "Hermès et les Charites" *BCH* 13 (1889), 467–76.

Lefkowitz, Mary R. *The Victory Ode.* Park Ridge, N. J., 1976.

Lendle, O. *Die 'Pandorasage' bei Hesiod, Textkritische und motivgeschichtliche Untersuchungen.* Würzburg, 1957.

Levet, J. *Le Vrai et le faux dans la pensée grecque archaïque.* Vol. I. Paris, 1976.

Levine, D. B. "Symposium and the Polis." In *Theognis of Megara: Poetry and the Polis,* ed. T. J. Figueira and G. Nagy. Baltimore/London, 1985, 176–96.

Lewis, J. M. "Eros and the *Polis* in Theognis Book II." In *Theognis of Megara: Poetry and the Polis,* ed. T. J. Figueira and G. Nagy. Baltimore/London, 1985, 197–222.

Lloyd, G. E. R. *Polarity and Analogy: Two Types of Argumentation in Early Greek Thought.* Cambridge, 1966.

Lloyd-Jones, H. *The Justice of Zeus².* Berkeley, 1983.

———. "Erinyes, Semnai Theai, Eumenides." In *Owls to Athens: Essays on Classical Subjects Presented to Sir Kenneth Dover,* ed. E. M. Craik. Oxford, 1990, 203–11.

Lomiento, L. "Bacchilide: una nuova traduzione e ancora un contributo agli studi sull' epinicio." *QUCC* 35 (1990), 121–32.

Long, A. A. "Morals and Values in Homer." *JHS* 90 (1970), 121–39.

Löw, O. "ΧΑΡΙΣ." Diss. Marburg, 1908.

Lundström, S. "Charitesia." *Eranos* 50 (1952), 138–41.

MacCary, W. Thomas. *Childlike Achilles: Ontogeny and Phylogeny in the Iliad.* New York, 1982.

MacLeod, C. W. *Homer, Iliad Book XXIV.* Cambridge, 1982a.

———. "Politics and the *Oresteia.*" *JHS* 102 (1982b), 124–44.

Maehler, H. ed. *Die Lieder des Bakchylides.* 2 vols. Leiden, 1982.

Maehler, H. post B. Snell. *Pindarus. Pars I Epinicia.* Leipzig, 1987.

Mauss, M. "Essai sur le don. Forme et raison de l'échange dans les sociétés archaïques." *Ann Soc* n.s. 1 (1923–24), 30–186.

Merkelbach, R. "Bakchylides 13, 205 und 59." *ZPE* 12 (1973), 90–91.

Morris, I. "Gift and Commodity in Archaic Greece." *Man* n.s. 21 (1986a) 1–17.

———. "The Use and Abuse of Homer." *CA* 5 (1986b), 81–138.

Most, G. W. *The Measures of Praise: Structure and Function in Pindar's Second Pythian and Seventh Nemean Odes. Hypomnemata* 83. Göttingen, 1985.

Motto, A. L., and J. R. Clark. "Isê Dais: The Honor of Achilles." *Arethusa* 2 (1969), 109–25.

Moussy, Claude. *Gratia et sa famille.* Paris, 1966.

Mugler, C. "La Lumière et la vision dans la poésie grecque." *REG* 73 (1960), 40–72.

Müller, K. O. *Orchomenos und die Minyer*. Breslau, 1844.

Müller, Max. *Essays on the Science of Language*. 2 vols. London, 1882.

Nagy, G. *The Best of the Achaeans: Concepts of the Hero in Archaic Greek Poetry*. Baltimore, 1979.

Neitzel, H. "Ἰστοτριβής (Aischylos, *Agamemnon* 1443)." *Glotta* 62 (1984), 157–61.

Newman, F. S. "Unity in the 14th Olympian." *RBPh* 52 (1974), 15–28.

Nilsson, M. P. *Griechische Feste von Religiöser Bedeutung*. Berlin, 1906.

———. *Geschichte der griechischen Religion*[3]. Munich, 1955.

Nisetich, Frank J. "Olympian 1.8–11: An Epinician Metaphor." *HSCP* 79 (1975), 55–68.

———, ed. *Pindar's Victory Songs*. Baltimore/London, 1980.

North, Helen. *Sophrosyne: Self-Knowledge and Self-Restraint in Greek Literature*. Ithaca, 1966.

Northrup, M. D. "The Use of Personification in Hesiod and the Pre-Socratics." Diss. Brown University, 1976.

Oliver, J. H. *Demokratia, the Gods and the Free World*. Baltimore, 1960.

Onians, R. B. *Origins of European Thought*. Cambridge, 1951.

Orsi, di Paolo. "ΕΡΜΑΤΑ ΤΡΙΓΛΗΝΑ ΜΟΡΟΕΝΤΑ." In *Strena Helbigiana*. Leipzig, 1898, 221–27.

Page, D. L. *History and the Homeric Iliad*. Berkeley/Los Angeles, 1959.

———, ed. *Aeschyli. Septem Quae Supersunt Tragoediae*. Oxford, 1972.

Palmer, L. R. "The Indo-European Origins of Justice." *TPS* (1950), 149–68.

———. *The Interpretation of Mycenaean Greek Texts*. Oxford, 1963.

Parry, A. "The Language of Achilles." *TAPA* 87 (1956), 1–7. (=*The Language of Achilles and Other Papers*, ed. H. Lloyd-Jones, Oxford, 1989, 1–7.)

Pearson, A. C., and W. G. Headlam, eds. (with additional notes from the papers of R. C. Jebb). *The Fragments of Sophocles*. Vol. II. Cambridge, 1917.

Pearson, L. *Popular Ethics in Ancient Greece*. Stanford, California, 1962.

Pfeiffer, R., ed. *Callimachus*. Oxford 1949.

———. "The Image of the Delian Apollo and Apolline Ethics." *JWI* 15 (1952), 20–32.

Picard, Ch. *Les Religions préhelléniques (Crète et Mycènes)*. Paris, 1948.

Podlecki, A. "Guest-Gifts and Nobodies in Odyssey 9." *Phoenix* 15 (1961), 125–33.

———. *The Political Background of Aeschylean Tragedy.* Ann Arbor, Mich., 1966.

Pokorny, J. *Indogermanisches etymologisches Wörterbuch.* Bern/ Munich, 1959.

Polanyi, K., C. Arensberg, and H. W. Pearson. *Trade and Market in the Early Empires: Economics in History and Theory.* Chicago, 1957.

Pope, M. "Merciful Heavens? A Question in Aeschylus' *Agamemnon*." *JHS* 94 (1974), 100–113.

Puech, Aimé. *L'Iliade d'Homère: étude et analyse.* Paris, 1948.

Radke, G. "Die ΛΕΥΚΑΙ ΚΟΡΑΙ." *Philologus* 92 (1937), 387–402.

Ramnoux, Clémence. *La Nuit et les enfants de la nuit dans la tradition grecque.* Paris, 1959.

Reinhardt, K. *Aischylos als Regisseur und Theologe.* Bern, 1949.

———. *Die Ilias und ihr Dichter.* Göttingen, 1961.

Richardson, N. J., ed. *The Homeric Hymn to Demeter.* Oxford, 1974.

Rist, Anna. *The Poems of Theocritus.* Chapel Hill, N.C., 1978.

Robbins, E. "The Concept of Inspiration in Greek Poetry from Homer to Pindar." Diss. Toronto, 1968.

———. "Cyrene and Cheiron: The Myth of Pindar's Ninth Pythian." *Phoenix* 32 (1978), 91–104.

———. "The Gifts of the Gods: Pindar's Third *Pythian*." *CQ* 40 (1990a), 307–18.

———. "Achilles to Thetis: *Iliad* 1, 365–412." *EMC /CV* 34 n.s. 9 (1990b), 1–15.

Robert, L. *Etudes épigraphiques et philologiques.* Paris, 1938.

Roberts, E. S., ed. *An Introduction to Greek Epigraphy.* Part 1, *The Archaic Inscriptions and the Greek Alaphabet.* Cambridge, 1887.

Rocchi, Maria. "Contributi Allo Culto Delle Charites I." *StudiClas* 18 (1979), 5–16.

———. "Contributi Allo Culto Delle Charites II." *StudiClas* 19 (1980), 19–28.

Rohde, Erwin. *Psyche: The Cult of Souls and Belief in Immortality among the Greeks.* London, 1925.

de Romilly, J. *La Douceur dans la pensée grecque.* Paris, 1979.

Rosenmeyer, T. G. *The Art of Aeschylus.* Berkeley/Los Angeles, 1982.

Rosner, J. A. "The Speech of Phoenix: *Il.* 9.434–605." *Phoenix* 30 (1976), 314–27.

Rouse, W. H. D. *Greek Votive Offerings, An Essay in the History of Greek Religion.* Cambridge, 1902.

Rudhardt, J. *Notions fondamentales de la pensée religieuse et actes constitutifs du culte dans la Grèce classique*. Geneva, 1958.

Sahlins, M. D. "On the sociology of primitive exchange." In his *Stone Age Economics*. Chicago, 1972, 185–275.

Sale, William. "Achilles and Heroic Values." *Arion* 2 (1963), 86–100.

Schachter, Albert. *The Cults of Boeotia*. London, 1981.

Schadewaldt, Wolfgang. *Der Aufbau des pindarischen Epinikion*. Halle, 1928a.

———. *Sappho, Welt und Dichtung: Dasein in der Liebe*. Halle, 1928b.

———. *Von Homers Welt und Werk, Aufsätze und Auslegungen zur homerischen Frage*, Stuttgart, 1944.

Schein, Seth L. *The Mortal Hero, an Introduction to Homer's Iliad*. Berkeley, 1984.

Schliemann, H. "Exploration of the Boeotian Orchomenos." *JHS* 2 (1881), 122–63.

Schmitt, R. *Dichtung und Dichtersprache in indogermanischer Zeit*. Weisbaden, 1967.

Schwarzenberg, E. *Die Grazien*. Bonn, 1966.

Scott, M. "Pity and Pathos in Homer." *A Class* 22 (1979), 1–14.

———. "Aidos and Nemesis." *A Class* 23 (1980), 13–36.

———. "Philos, Philotes and Xenia." *A Class* 25 (1982), 1–20.

———. "Charis in Homer and the Homeric Hymns." *A Class* 24 (1983), 1–13.

Scully, S. E. "Philia and Charis in Euripidean Tragedy." Diss. Toronto, 1973.

Segal, C. P. "God and Man in Pindar's First and Third Olympian Odes." *HSCP* 68 (1964), 211–64.

———. "Messages to the Underworld." *AJP* 106 (1985), 203–6.

Seng, H. "Τὰ δίκαια beim Symposion." *QUCC* 30 (1988) 123–31.

Sheppard, J. T. *The Pattern of the Iliad*. London, 1922.

Slater, W. J. "Pindar's House." *GRBS* 12 (1971), 141–52.

———. "Peace, the Symposium and the Poet." *ICS* 6 (1981), 205–14.

Smith, K. F., ed. *The Elegies of Albius Tibullus*. New York/Cincinnati, 1913.

Smyth, H. W. *Greek Grammar*. 1920. Cambridge, Mass.

Snell, Bruno. *The Discovery of the Mind, the Greek Origins of European Thought*[2]. Cambridge, Mass., 1953.

Snyder, J. "The Web of Song: Weaving Imagery in Homer and the Lyric Poets." *CJ* 76 (1981), 193–96.

Solmsen, Friedrich. *Hesiod and Aeschylus*. Ithaca, N.Y., 1949.

Sommerstein, A., ed. *Aeschylus. Eumenides*. Cambridge, 1989.

Sourvinou-Inwood, C. "A Series of Erotic Pursuits: Images and Meanings." *JHS* 107 (1987), 131–53.

Stanford, W. B. *Greek Metaphor: Studies in Theory and Practice.* Oxford, 1936.

Stenzel, Julius. *Philosophie der Sprache, Handbuch der Philosophie.* Munich/Berlin, 1934.

———. *Platon der Erzieher.* Hamburg, 1961.

Thomson, G. *Aeschylus and Athens: A Study in the Social Origins of Drama.* London, 1941.

Tod, M. C. "Greek Inscriptions at Cairness House." *JHS* 54 (1934), 159–62.

Treu, Max. *Von Homer zur Lyrik: Wandlungen des griechischen Weltbildes im Spiegel der Sprache.* Munich, 1955.

———. "Licht und Leuchtendes in der archaïschen griechischen Poesie." *Stud Gen* 18 (1965), 83–97.

Usener, Hermann. *Götternamen.* Frankfurt, 1948.

van Groningen, B. A. *Pindare au banquet: Les fragments des scolies, édités avec commentaire.* Leiden, 1960.

———, ed. *Theognis, le premier livre.* Amsterdam, 1966.

Vatin, C. "Poinê, Timê, Thoiê dans le droit homérique." *Ktema* 7 (1982), 275–80.

Ventris, Michael, and John Chadwick. *Documents in Mycenaean Greek.* Cambridge, 1956.

Verdenius, W. J. "Parmenides B 2, 3." *Mnem* ser. 4, 15 (1962), 237.

———. *A Commentary on Hesiod, Works and Days, vv. 1–382.* Leiden, 1985.

———. *Commentaries on Pindar, Mnem* Suppl. Vol. I, Leiden, 1987.

Verrall, A. W. *The Eumenides of Aeschylus.* London, 1908.

———, ed. *ΑΙΣΧΥΛΟΥ ΕΥΜΕΝΙΔΕΣ: The 'Eumenides' of Aeschylus.* London, 1908.

Vetta, M., ed. *Theognis Elegiarum Liber.* Rome, 1980.

Vivante, P. *The Homeric Imagination, A Study of Homer's Poetic Perception of Reality.* Bloomington, Ill., 1970.

Vlastos, Gregory. "Equality and Justice in Early Greek Cosmologies." *CP* 42 (1947), 156–78.

Wace, A. J. B., and F. H. Stubbings. *A Companion to Homer.* London, 1962.

Wade-Gery, H. T. *The Poet of the Iliad.* Cambridge, 1952.

West, M. L., ed. *Hesiod. Theogony.* Oxford, 1966.

———. "Burning Sappho." *Maia* 22 (1970), 307–30.

———. *Studies in Greek Elegy and Iambus.* Berlin, 1974.

———, ed. *Hesiod. Works and Days.* Oxford, 1978.

————, ed. *Aeschyli Tragoediae cum incerti poetae Prometheo*. Stuttgart, 1990.

Whitman, Cedric H. *Homer and the Heroic Tradition*. Cambridge, Mass., 1958.

von Wilamowitz-Moellendorff, Ulrich. *Die Ilias und Homer*. Berlin, 1916.

————. *Pindaros*. Berlin, 1922.

Winnington-Ingram, R. P. "A Religious Function of Greek Tragedy." *JHS* 74 (1954), 16–24.

Woodbury, L. "The Seal of Theognis." *Studies in Honour of Gilbert Norwood*. Toronto, 1952, 20–41 (Reprinted in *Leonard E. Woodbury, Collected Writings*, Atlanta, Ga., 1991, 26–45).

————. "Equinox at Acragas: Pindar, *Ol.* 2.61–62." *TAPA* 97 (1966), 597–616 (= *Collected Writings*, 151–67).

————. "Pindar and the Mercenary Muse: *Isthm.* 2.1–13." *TAPA* 99 (1968), 527–42 (= *Collected Writings*, 188–200).

————. "Truth and the Song: Bacchylides 3.96–98." *Phoenix* 23 (1969), 331–35 (=*Collected Writings*, 201–5).

————. "Apollo's First Love: Pindar, *Pyth.* 9.26ff." *TAPA* 103 (1972), 561–78 (= *Collected Writings*, 233–43).

————. "The Gratitude of the Locrian Maiden: Pindar, *Pyth.* 2.18–20." *TAPA* 108 (1978), 285–99 (= *Collected Writings*, 271–85).

————. "The Victor's Virtues: Pindar, *Isth.* 1.32ff." *TAPA* 111 (1981), 237–56 (= *Collected Writings*, 376–95).

————. "Cyrene and the Τελευτά of Marriage in Pindar's Ninth Pythian Ode." *TAPA* 112 (1982), 245–58 (= *Collected Writings*, 396–409).

————. "Ibycus and Polycrates." *Phoenix* 39 (1985), 193–220 (= *Collected Writings*, 410–38).

Young, David C. *Three Odes of Pindar, a Literary Study of Pythian 11, Pythian 3, and Olympian 7, Mnemosyne Supplementum Nonum*. Leiden, 1968.

Zielinski, T. "Charis and Charites." *CQ* 18 (1924), 158–63.

Zuntz, G. *The Political Plays of Euripides*. Manchester, 1955.

INDEX LOCORUM ANTIQUORUM

Bacchylides (*cont.*)
8.20: **100**
9.2: **114**
9.83: **102**
10.39–42: **112**
11.3–5: **164**
14.19–21: **163**
15.48–49: **114**
19.1–11: **95–96**
19.11: **103**

CALLIMACHUS

Hymn to Artemis

129–31: **54**

DIONYSIUS CHALCUS

1: **83**

EURIPIDES

Alcestis
299: **154**
659–61: **153**
840–42: **154**
1072–74: **154**
1087: **154**
1101: **154**
1108: **154**

Hecuba
132: **157**
138–40: **157**
249–50: **158**
272–76: **158**
309–20: **158**
830–32: **158**
855–56: **158**
874: **159**
1175–76: **159**
1202–3: **159**
1211–13: **160**
1236–37: **160**

Helen
900–902: **155**
917–23: **155**
940–41: **155**
1197: **156**
1234: **156**
1273: **156**
1281: **156**
1378: **156**
1397: **157**
1402: **157**
1411: **157**
1420: **157**
1449–50: **157**

Hippolytus
202: **65**
1279–80: **54**

Fragments (Nauck)
736.3–6: **75**

HESIOD

Opera et Dies
60–82: **36f.**
73: **37, 57**
75: **57**
190–93: **26**
190: **77**
192: **26**
231: **39**
349–51: **80**
709: **25, 161**
719–23: **24–25**
722: **82**

Theogony
65: **39**
77: **39**
92: **25**
503–5: **18**
570–84: **37f.**
902: **40**

GENERAL INDEX

acharis charis, 39n.24, 81, 128, 136f., 140, 152, 153, 155
Adkins, A.W.H., 14n.4, 22n.16
agathoi, 78f.
Aglaia, 34, 36–40, 42, 51, 53, 117
agnos, 62 and n. 15
aidôs, 11, 147–48; and *charis*, 32–33, 69–70, 73, 109–10, 148; from Charis, 109; "disarming" effect, 25–26 and n. 20, 147–48; on eyes, 32–33 and n. 25, 66; loss of, 81; between lovers, 69f., 148; among members of a community, 73f., 81, 149; toward parents, 153; and *sophrosynê*, 77; through speech, 25; at the symposium, 82, 149
alatheia, 100, 101, 102, 114
Alcmaeon, 65n. 20
Anaximander, 20n.12
Apatouria, 44
Aphrodite, 67, 69, 70–71, 113. *See also under* Charites
aretê, 22n.16, 91, 101
Arieti, A., 14n.4, 21n.14
Aristotle: 5, 9, 49n.19, 80–81 and n. 8
Athena, 142f., 148
Austin, N., 84n.12, 85n.15
Auxesia, 45
Auxo, 54 and n. 28

Barrett, W. S., 28n.22
Bassett, S. E., 14n.3
Bell, J., 45n.8, 85n.14, 121n. 49
Benveniste, E., 16n.7
Bernardini, P. A., 118n.43
Bielohlawek, K., 82n.10
Blech, M., 93n.3
Blundell, M. W., 10

Borgeaud, W., 52n.26
Bowra, C. M., 14n.2, 106n.24
Bremer, D., 35n.27, 117n.41
Brown, A. L., 146n.20
Brown, C. G., 35n.28, 36n.30, 59n.7, 91n.2, 111n.34
Buckler, J., 47n.12
Bundy, E. L., 105n.22
Burkert, W., 47nn.13 and 15, 140n.14, 145n.18
Burnett, A. P., 63n.16, 99n.13
Bury, J. B., 162
Buxton, R.G.A., 141n.16

Calame, C., 45n.5
Campbell, D. A., 62n.14
Chadwick, J., 37n.33
chairein. See *charis*, etymology of
Chantraine, P., 4n.1, 21n.14
chara. See *charis*, etymology of
charieis, 37n.32, 38, 61, 110n.32
charin oida, charin eidenai, 5 and n. 2, 6, 79
charis: and *aidôs* (see *aidôs*); and beauty, 10, 11, 67, 75–76, 98, 109–10 and n. 32, 129 and n. 6, 147–49; bonding through, 15, 28f., 77, 107 and n.27, 108n.30, 149; and charm, 98 and n. 13, 113–14, 147; between children and parents, 27 and n. 21; chthonic powers of, 46, 139 and n. 13; and civility, 72, 81–82, 86, 118–19, 121, 123; and desire, 56f., 61–65, 67f., 97, 110, 116, 134–35 and n. 9, 148; "disarming" effects of, 11, 25, 31–33, 113–15, 148–49; as divine favor, 90, 97, 113, 115, 117, 126, 128, 130, 144–45, 157, 161;